MATT CHRISTOPHER®

On the Court with....
Michael Jordan

MATT CHRISTOPHER®

On the Court with....
Michael Jordan

Text by Glenn Stout

LITTLE, BROWN AND COMPANY

New York ∾ Boston

Little, Brown and Company
Time Warner Book Group
1271 Avenue of the Americas, New York, NY 10020
Visit our Web site at www.lb-kids.com

First Edition

Matt Christopher® is a registered trademark of
Catherine M. Christopher

Cover photograph by Bill Smith/Bill Smith Photography

Library of Congress Cataloging-in-Publication Data

Stout, Glenn.
  Michael Jordan / Glenn Stout.
       p.   cm.
  Summary: Examines the life and basketball career of the high-
scoring player with the Chicago Bulls, who made a brief attempt to
play minor-league baseball in 1994.
  ISBN 0-316-13792-8 (pb)
  1. Jordan, Michael — Juvenile literature. 2. Basketball
players — United States — Biography — Juvenile literature.
[1. Jordan, Michael. 2. Basketball players. 3. Afro-
Americans — Biography.]   I. Title.
GV884J67C57 1996
796.323 092—dc20
[B]   96-971

20 19 18 17 16 15 14

COM-MO

Printed in the United States of America

To my daughter, Pamela

Contents

Chapter One:
1963–1981

From "the Rack" to the Tar Heels

Michael Jordan defies the law of gravity.

At least that's what opponents, teammates, and fans have been saying for years. Since Michael Jordan first burst upon the scene as a freshman at the University of North Carolina, basketball fans around the world have marveled at his talent.

So what does Michael Jordan do that's so special? Every time he touches the basketball there is a good chance you will see him do something you have never seen before. Sometimes Michael will launch himself from the free throw line, lift the ball high above his head, and make a thunderous jam through the hoop. Other times he leaps and seems to hang in the air. As defenders try unsuccessfully to knock the ball from his hand, Michael calmly brings it back down and flips it underhand toward the basket, where it kisses the glass and falls through for two more points. Sometimes he'll even start on one side of the basket, jump, spin 360 degrees through the air, come out the other side, flick the ball over his head, and catch nothing but net.

After a great play, Michael Jordan seems to freeze in space for a moment, sweat glistening off his shaved head, mouth wide open, his tongue curled around his lower lip. The crowd can only look on in wide-eyed disbelief.

Then Michael Jordan is in motion again, a look of wild surprise upon his face as the crowd roars and his opponents roll their eyes and shake their heads. He flashes a quick smile as if to say, "How about that?" glances up toward his family in the stands, and sprints back up court, ready to do it all once more. Air Jordan has struck again.

But Michael Jordan was not born with the ability to play basketball better than any other human being on the planet. When he first started playing, he couldn't dribble the ball without bouncing it off his foot. His shots didn't even make it to the basket. Dunking a basketball was just a dream.

So how did Michael Jordan become so good?

Through hard work and practice. He knows that people aren't born great athletes; they make themselves great athletes. Through hard work, practice, and determination, the best athletes learn to take advantage of their physical gifts and develop them to the fullest. Great players love competition and always strive to become better.

That is how Michael Jordan became perhaps the greatest basketball player of all time. While he is blessed with tremendous physical skill, he also worked extremely hard to develop the talent he was born with. Each time he failed, he tried again and tried harder. Each time he succeeded, he gave himself another goal to try to achieve. Even today, Michael Jordan still tries to improve.

Michael Jordan was taught those valuable lessons by his parents, James and Deloris Jordan. Both of Michael's parents were born on small farms in Wallace, North Carolina. Their parents — Michael's grandparents — were sharecroppers: farmers who paid the rent on their small plots of land by sharing the crops they produced with the landowners.

While Michael's parents always had enough to eat, both families were poor. Sharecropping is hard work. Michael's parents both dreamed of a better life for themselves and their future children.

James and Deloris met in high school after attending — what else? — a basketball game. The first time they met, James told Deloris, "I'm gonna marry you someday." A few years later, he did.

Most fans already know that Michael Jordan grew up in North Carolina and attended the University of North Carolina before turning professional and playing for the Chicago Bulls in the National Basketball Association (NBA). Few people realize, however, that Michael Jordan was born not in North Carolina but in Brooklyn, New York.

After he graduated from high school, James Jordan served in the air force for several years, then went to work for General Electric. The Jordan family grew quickly, and soon the young couple had three children — James Ronald, Deloris, and Larry. In 1963, James brought his young family to Brooklyn so he could attend a General Electric training school. Michael was born on February 17, 1963, while the family was living in Brooklyn.

With four children to raise, James and Deloris

worked hard to provide for their family. As soon as James completed the training course, the Jordans returned to North Carolina. A year later, Michael's younger sister, Roslyn, was born. As soon as the children were old enough, Michael's mother went to work in a bank to help support the family.

When the Jordans first returned to North Carolina, they lived in a small rented house. But James Jordan wanted better for his family. He and his wife saved their money and purchased a six-and-a-half-acre plot of land in Wilmington, North Carolina. James decided to build a home for his family. He spent evenings and weekends constructing a small but comfortable brick house. Sometimes he took his children with him. The young Jordans helped their father carry bricks and mortar and learned the value of hard work firsthand. Brick by brick, they saw the result of their labor.

James Jordan taught his children to play hard, too. When he was in high school, he had played guard on his school's basketball team, and he loved many sports. So James encouraged his children to play sports and games of all kinds. He thought it was much safer for the boys to be playing sports than running around Wilmington looking for trouble.

There was always some kind of game going on at the Jordan house. If James Ronald and Larry weren't in the yard playing football or throwing a baseball back and forth, they were crowded around the kitchen table playing checkers or a board game. Deloris Jordan later told people that the only time the boys stopped competing against each other was when they ate dinner.

Everyone in the family loved competition. When James Jordan played with his sons, he didn't ease off and allow them to win. The boys had to earn their success on their own. As the youngest son in the Jordan household, Michael was usually on the losing end when playing against his brothers.

At first, baseball was Michael Jordan's favorite sport. James Jordan was a big fan and he taught Michael to throw and hit. In Little League, Michael pitched, and played shortstop and outfield. He threw several no-hitters, and his team won the championship.

Then Larry fell in love with the game of basketball. To help his son, James Jordan built something very special in the backyard. At opposite ends of the yard, he put up two wooden backboards and two baskets. Then he gave the boys a basketball.

In only a few days, the Jordan boys played so much they wore down the grass in the yard between the two baskets. The dirt became as hard and smooth as concrete. Although they knew it was no Chicago Stadium, the Jordan boys thought their backyard court was the best in the world. They called it "the Rack."

Larry and Michael spent hours each day playing one-on-one at the Rack. At first, Larry beat Michael every single time.

While Larry gave Michael the occasional tip, he never just let his younger brother win. Michael learned quickly that he would have to earn each victory.

Although Larry was only five foot six, he towered over young Michael. He dribbled the ball better than Michael, shot the ball over Michael's raised arms, and jumped higher. Michael watched in wonder as his older brother soared through the air. Larry eventually became the first member of the Jordan family to dunk the basketball. But Michael was de-

7

termined. He didn't give up. Everyone in the family started calling him "Rabbit" because of the way he bounded back and forth after Larry.

Michael spent hours at the Rack practicing shooting, dribbling back and forth, and trying to reach over his brother's arms. Without even realizing it, he started sticking his tongue out and curling it around his lower lip as he practiced. His father did the very same thing when he was concentrating hard.

Despite the long hours of practice, Michael still wasn't as good as his brother. When he and Larry joined a youth basketball league, Larry was a big star. Michael was just another member of the team.

The Jordan boys were playing for fun. Like other kids, they dreamed of becoming professional athletes, but they never really thought those dreams would come true. Homework was always more important at the Jordan house than basketball. The one sure way to get into trouble was to fall behind in school. In order to play ball, all the Jordan children had to excel in school. They loved to play so much that James and Deloris rarely had a difficult time making sure the children worked hard at school.

By the time Michael entered D. C. Virgo Junior High School, he was a good all-around athlete. While Larry starred in the backcourt for the Laney High School Buccaneers basketball team, Michael played quarterback on the junior high football team, guard on the basketball team, and pitched and played outfield on the baseball team. Michael was a good athlete for his age, but no one was predicting greatness. Besides, Michael stood only five feet five inches tall.

None of the Jordans was very tall. Michael's father and his brother Larry were barely five foot six. But something happened to Michael. He just kept growing.

By the time Michael entered high school, he stood five foot ten. During his sophomore year, he quarterbacked the junior varsity football team and ran some track. He also tried out for the varsity basketball team.

It may seem amazing, but Michael Jordan didn't make the team. He was cut and placed on the junior varsity. When Laney coach Clifton Herring told Michael he was putting him on the JV team, Michael's eyes stung with disappointment. He was embarrassed and hurt. One of Michael's best friends, also a sophomore, had made the varsity. Michael thought about quitting the game of basketball altogether.

But he didn't. Instead, Michael was determined to become the best player on the junior varsity team.

Michael didn't know it, but Coach Herring secretly thought he was good enough to play for the varsity. The coach simply wanted him to get more experience, and he would have a greater opportunity to play and improve with the JV team.

The extra playing time helped. Over the course of the JV season, Michael became a little faster and a little quicker than most of his teammates. He jumped higher and seemed to stay in the air just a little bit longer. His jump shot became more and more accurate. In practice, his teammates couldn't keep up with him. Neither could their junior varsity opponents.

Michael averaged 28 points per game as point guard for the JV team. Near the end of the season, Michael hoped he would be added to the varsity squad for the state tournament.

The varsity team had had a winning season and

hoped to do well in the state basketball tournament. But when Coach Herring announced the squad, he selected one of Michael's JV teammates, Leroy Smith, to join the team for the tournament.

Coach Herring knew Michael hustled on the court and could score. But the varsity team needed rebounding in the tournament, not scoring. Coach Herring chose Smith because he was six foot five. Michael was disappointed again.

The day the team was scheduled to travel to the regionals, Michael heard the team manager was ill. He wanted to be a part of the team so badly that he volunteered to take the manager's place. He rode to the game with the team and got inside the gym carrying the equipment. While his friends played in the state tournament, Michael sat on the end of the bench in his street clothes, passing out towels and yelling words of encouragement.

The time Michael spent as team manager wasn't wasted. He learned from the experience and later told an interviewer, "I vowed to myself to never let that happen again." From that moment on, Michael was determined to *play*. Each day that summer he played basketball in his backyard for hours on end.

By the beginning of his junior year, all Michael's hard work began to have an effect. It was as if the running and leaping Michael had been doing had somehow stretched out his body. The slight five-foot-ten-inch sophomore had turned into a powerful six-foot-three-inch junior. His father later said, "I think Michael just willed himself to grow."

The added height made Michael an imposing figure on the court. Few players his size had his speed and grace. At basketball tryouts, Michael Jordan made the varsity squad easily and was named starting point guard. In this position, Michael was expected to run the offense and do his share of scoring. His teammates would look to him to provide leadership.

Yet when the season began, Michael Jordan struggled. He was rushing everything and forcing his play instead of allowing the game to bring opportunities to him. As a result, he was making too many turnovers and taking wild shots. Then, after making a mistake or two, Michael would try to do everything himself and make even more mistakes.

By the time Christmas came around, Michael was a disappointment not only to himself but to Coach

Herring and his teammates. He knew that if he didn't start playing better soon, Coach Herring would try someone else at point guard.

Laney was entered in a holiday basketball tournament. In the first game, Michael struggled again. Nevertheless, Laney won and reached the tournament finals against its archrival, New Hanover High School.

The teams were evenly matched. For most of the game, neither was able to pull ahead. Michael was playing pretty well, but Laney needed someone to do something more.

Michael Jordan became that someone. As time ran down in the fourth quarter, all the hours of practice and hard work started to pay off. Michael Jordan simply took over the game.

He was unstoppable. When New Hanover had the ball, there was Michael, hounding the dribbler and stealing the pass. When Laney had possession, Michael's teammates simply threw him the ball and got out of the way. They watched in awe as he slashed to the hoop, spun in the air, and put the ball in the basket over and over again. The crowd was going crazy.

13

With only seconds left in the game, Laney still trailed by a point. Once more, Michael's teammates passed him the ball. The New Hanover defense collapsed toward the basket, expecting Michael to drive to the hoop.

Michael started to drive, but seeing the defense packed in, he pulled up and calmly launched a fifteen-foot jumper. The ball was still in the air when the buzzer sounded. The spectators held their breath.

Swish! Two points! Laney won!

A quick glance at the scorekeeper's sheet showed something remarkable — Michael Jordan had scored Laney High's last 15 points!

From that moment, Michael was a different player. Throughout the rest of the season, whenever Laney needed something — a basket, a rebound, a pass to an open player — Michael was the player who came through.

Michael's perseverance and attitude made an impression on Coach Herring, but he thought his star player had a chance to become even better. In his opinion, Michael needed more experience and would benefit from playing against better competition. With college scouts beginning to ask about the lanky point guard, Coach Herring and an assistant coach at the University of North Carolina recommended that Michael be invited to a summer basketball camp known as the Five Star camp.

The Five Star camp, held in Pittsburgh, Pennsylvania, is one of the most important basketball camps for high school players in the country. Over a three-week period, players receive intense instruction from top coaches and scrimmage against each other over and over again. Scouts from colleges all over the country attend. Only the very best players in the United States are invited to participate. Most players go to the camp thinking they are great, only to return home realizing they have a lot of work left to do.

Michael was stunned when he received his invitation to Five Star. He wasn't sure that he belonged there. And when Coach Herring told him that some college scouts thought he could play Division I basketball, the highest level in college hoops, Michael couldn't believe it. No player from Laney High

School had ever played Division I before. Michael was determined not to let this opportunity pass him by.

At the beginning of the camp, hardly anyone knew who Michael Jordan was. But playing against better competition made Michael a better player. He hated to lose and did whatever it took to win. At the end of his first week, Michael had won five trophies and was the most talked-about player in the camp.

College recruiters who had come to Five Star to scout other players began paying attention to Michael. They couldn't believe that some player they had never heard of was outplaying the best high school players in the country. They kept waiting for Michael to fail.

He didn't. If anything, Michael played even better the second week, and won four more trophies. By the end of the third week, the colleges were very interested in Michael Jordan. Here, perhaps, was a player worthy of a college scholarship.

Michael returned home from Five Star excited and full of confidence. Before, he had never even considered the possibility that he could get to college playing basketball. Now that he knew he had a chance to earn a scholarship, Michael Jordan became absolutely possessed by basketball.

At the beginning of his senior year, Michael practically moved into the high school gym. Before school started, while it was still dark outside, he went to the gym and practiced. After school, long after it was dark, he practiced some more. When basketball season started, Michael practiced with both the varsity and the junior varsity teams. When he returned home late at night, he shot baskets in the backyard or convinced Larry to play one-on-one. Now Michael usually won.

Then Michael went a little overboard. One day, he cut biology class and went to the gym instead. When he didn't get caught, he cut class again the next day.

After about a week of cutting classes, Michael's absence was finally noticed. In the middle of the school day, the principal called Michael's home looking for him. James Jordan answered the phone, and when he was told Michael was missing from class, he asked the principal, "Did you check the gym?" Sure enough, Michael was playing basketball. Michael might have been a big high school basket-

17

ball star, but that didn't make him an exception to school rules. The principal suspended Michael from school.

James and Deloris Jordan were not happy with their son. They didn't care how good Michael was at playing basketball. They knew that unless he was a good student, too, all his athletic talent would go to waste. James Jordan sat Michael down and told him straight out, "The way you're going, you'll never get to college."

Michael swallowed hard. He realized his father was right. He knew he had to work just as hard in the classroom as he did on the court in order to reach his dreams. A player who was all moves but no brain would never go far. Michael stopped cutting class, and his grades soon improved dramatically.

Ever since he had returned from basketball camp, college coaches had been trying to convince Michael to attend their schools. Coaches called the Jordan house at all hours to talk to Michael, and every day the mailbox was full of letters telling him how great this or that school was and how much he'd enjoy playing for them. It started to get a little hectic.

After his suspension, Michael knew he couldn't afford to have any more distractions during his senior year. He decided to select a college before the basketball season started.

At first, Michael thought about attending North Carolina State. A few years before, NC State had won the National Collegiate Athletic Association (NCAA) championship. Their best player, David Thompson, had been Michael's favorite player.

But when Michael went to visit colleges, he was surprised to discover that he preferred the University of North Carolina (UNC), NC State's biggest rival. The campus was gorgeous, and the North Carolina coach, Dean Smith, had one of the best reputations in the country. Coach Smith was more than just a basketball coach. He was a good teacher, too. His teams were successful, and he tried to make sure each player received his degree. Some North Carolina players had gone on to become NBA stars, and even those who didn't had become successes off the basketball court.

Just before his last high school basketball season started, Michael announced he would attend the University of North Carolina.

With that decision out of the way, many people wondered if Michael would take it easy his senior year. He didn't. He still practiced as hard as ever and still found the time to do his schoolwork.

Michael Jordan was one of the best players in the state. When the Laney team took the court that year, the opposition usually assigned two or three players just to guard Michael.

It didn't matter. Michael kept getting better and better. Despite being challenged every time he touched the ball, he averaged almost 28 points per game.

Michael Jordan had learned his lessons well. High school was over. He was ready for college.

Chapter Two:
1981–1984

"Mike's a Good Player."

In the fall of 1981, Michael Jordan officially enrolled at the University of North Carolina in Chapel Hill, North Carolina. He was anxious and excited when he arrived on campus. While he had been a big star back in Wilmington, every player on the North Carolina team had been a big high school star. Michael wondered if he was good enough to play.

The University of North Carolina basketball program was one of the most successful in the nation. The basketball team, nicknamed the Tar Heels, played in the Atlantic Coast Conference (ACC), one of the best college basketball leagues in the country. Almost every season, the Tar Heels challenged for the league championship and earned a place in the NCAA tournament. One year earlier, the Tar Heels had reached the finals of the tournament, losing to the University of Indiana in the championship game.

North Carolina coach Dean Smith was one of the most respected coaches in the country. His Tar Heel teams were known for their strong fundamental play, defense, and teamwork. There was no place in the Tar Heel lineup for a selfish player.

The first few days at Chapel Hill, Michael wondered if he had made the right decision. He was overwhelmed.

College classes were very different from high school — and a lot more difficult! He knew he would have to study hard. Then, when he first met his teammates on the Tar Heels, it seemed as if every player was better than anyone Michael had ever played against. Two Tar Heels, forward James Worthy and center Sam Perkins, were All-Americans. Michael was homesick, and his confidence was shaken.

Fortunately, Michael's roommate, fellow Tar Heel Buzz Peterson, helped Michael adjust to college life. The two first met in high school while attending special camps and playing in all-star games.

It didn't take long for Buzz and Michael to become close friends, a fact that surprised many people. Buzz was white. Michael was black. Both played guard and knew they would compete for the same position in the Tar Heel lineup.

But Michael and Buzz had so much in common they hardly paid any attention to their differences. They loved basketball and talked about the game late into the night. They kept on each other about their schoolwork, too. They became such good friends that within a few months they even began wearing each other's clothing!

One day, just before official practice began, Michael went to the North Carolina gym looking for a pickup basketball game. James Worthy, Sam Perkins, and other veteran members of the team were already on the court playing with Al Wood and Mitch Kupchak, former UNC stars who were now in the NBA.

Worthy and Perkins saw their freshman teammate-to-be standing on the sidelines and invited him to play.

When Michael stepped on the court, his knees

were shaking. He was so nervous he could hardly think. He kept telling himself to let the game come to him.

It was only a pickup game, but Michael didn't want to make any mistakes. He played carefully. He wasn't hurting his team, but he wasn't helping much, either.

Then, with the game tied, the ball landed in Michael's hand. All of a sudden, he forgot about being careful. Without thinking, he drove to the basket.

Al Wood glided over in front of Michael, then jumped to block his shot. At the same time, UNC backup center Geoff Crompton, seven feet tall, came at Michael from the side.

Michael jumped, holding the ball in one hand.

Wood reached up to block his shot, but Michael somehow slid past him in the air. Crompton stretched out his arms, but even he couldn't reach Michael.

Crash! Michael slammed the ball through the hoop. The game was over. Michael's team won.

The other players stopped in their tracks and stared at Michael for a second before they started whooping and hollering, slapping him on the back, and putting their arms around his shoulders. A big grin broke out on Michael's face. He knew he belonged.

When official practice began, Michael learned there was only one open spot in the starting lineup, at guard. Few expected a freshman, even Michael Jordan, to start for Coach Smith. Most players took at least a year to learn Smith's system, and Smith preferred to play experienced ballplayers. Only three freshmen had ever started a game for Coach Smith.

But Michael Jordan had an advantage. The North Carolina offense was identical to the one used by Laney High. In the first few weeks of practice, Michael played well. Smith noticed that no one on the team could guard Michael one-on-one.

Then Michael twisted an ankle and missed two weeks of practice. He wasn't able to play again until just a few days before Carolina's first game of the season, against Kansas. Although his ankle was fully healed, Michael didn't expect to play very much.

Before the game, the UNC players slowly filtered into the locker room. The veterans went straight to their lockers and started getting dressed, joking with one another and filling the room with laughter.

Michael was nervous. Before he went to his locker, he walked nonchalantly, head down, over to a blackboard in the locker room. Coach Smith had told the players the starting lineup would appear on the blackboard.

Michael took a deep breath and quickly glanced up at the board.

He saw his name! He had made the starting lineup!

When Michael ran out on the court for warm-up, he hardly felt his feet touch the court. More than 11,000 fans packed the stands, and the game was being broadcast all over the East Coast. Michael tried to stay calm.

But when the game started, Michael still felt butterflies in his stomach. The first time he touched the ball, he tossed up a jump shot.

The shot missed, but as the ball caromed off the basket, Michael's butterflies disappeared. He stopped being nervous and began playing basketball. The next time he got the ball, he drove to the baseline, leaped above two defenders, and sank a short jumper. He was on his way.

North Carolina won, 74–67. Everyone on the team had played well, and Michael had scored 12 points.

After the game, a reporter asked Michael's teammate, guard Jimmy Black, for his opinion of the young freshman. Said Black, "Mike's a good player."

Good soon became great. Two weeks later, in a game against ninth-ranked Tulsa, Michael was nearly unstoppable. In only 22 minutes of play, he hit 11 of 15 shots for 22 points. Michael also stole the ball four times and blocked a shot. UNC beat Tulsa, 78–70.

Everyone in college basketball was beginning to take notice of Michael Jordan. Even Michael was finally beginning to realize how good he was. He told one reporter, "When I first got here, I thought everybody was a superstar. Now I realize I'm as good as everybody else."

With Michael, James Worthy, and Sam Perkins leading the way, the Tar Heels tore through the remainder of the season, finishing with a record of

24–2. They won the ACC championship and the conference tournament. Entering the NCAA tournament, the Tar Heels were ranked number one in the nation.

But being number one was no guarantee of success. A lot of people expected North Carolina to fail. While Coach Smith had taken the Tar Heels to the championship games of the tournament three times before, North Carolina had lost each time. Some people wondered if a team coached by Smith could win the championship.

In their first tournament game, against lightly regarded James Madison University, the Tar Heels struggled and barely eked out a 52–50 victory. That game was representative of the entire tournament, as North Carolina narrowly defeated Alabama, Villanova, and Houston to make the finals.

Their opponents in the championship game were the Hoyas of Georgetown University. Georgetown had a great team and was particularly strong on defense. The freshman center, seven-foot-tall Patrick Ewing, was considered by many to be the best freshman player in the nation, even better than Michael Jordan.

The game was played before 61,612 fans in the Louisiana Superdome in New Orleans. Millions more watched the game on television.

The first four times North Carolina brought the ball down the court and shot, Patrick Ewing jumped up and swatted the ball away from the basket. He was called for goaltending each time, but he was sending North Carolina a message: Nothing was going to come easy.

The two teams battled back and forth the entire game. Neither was able to open up a big lead. Each team challenged every shot. Every loose ball ended with a half-dozen players on the court scrambling to pick it up.

Then, with less than a minute to play, Georgetown guard Eric "Sleepy" Floyd hit a running jump shot to give the Hoyas a 62–61 lead. Coach Smith called a time-out.

In the Georgetown huddle, Hoya coach John Thompson told his players to watch for James Worthy and Sam Perkins. Worthy had already scored 28 points, and Thompson thought Worthy would probably take the last shot.

But Coach Smith of North Carolina was thinking

one step ahead of his counterpart. He expected Georgetown to blanket both Worthy and Perkins. Smith decided that Michael Jordan would take the last shot.

The move made sense but was also a little risky. While Michael had a hot hand and had scored two important baskets in the last few minutes, he was also a freshman. Smith hoped that Michael could take the pressure. He called the play, and as the Tar Heel huddle broke up, Smith leaned over to Michael, cupped his hand over his ear, and said, "Make it, Michael." Michael Jordan gave his coach a quick nod.

Jimmy Black inbounded the ball to Jordan at mid-court, and the two guards passed the ball back and forth as they sized up the Georgetown defense. When a Hoya player challenged Black for the ball, he set the play in motion, snapping the ball to forward Matt Doherty at the top of the key.

As the Georgetown defense started to collapse toward the basket, Doherty returned the ball to Black on the right side. Then, when the Georgetown defense swung toward him, Black took one dribble, feinted a pass inside, then tossed the ball crosscourt to Michael on the left side.

Georgetown was caught off guard. Underneath the basket, James Worthy and Sam Perkins were well covered. Michael was open.

The entire Georgetown team stopped and surged in his direction. Michael Jordan, seventeen feet from the basket, calmly jumped into the air.

At the top of his leap, he hung in the air, then flicked the ball toward the basket with his right hand. The shot arched up high and long. Time seemed to stop as the ball reached its peak and started to curve back down.

The ball snapped through the basket.

Two points! The Tar Heels took the lead, 63–62!

A few seconds later, Georgetown threw the ball away and North Carolina ran out the clock. The Tar Heels were NCAA champions!

Michael Jordan was a hero. Back in North Carolina, Tar Heel fans started referring to the play as simply "the Shot." Everyone knew that meant Michael's game-ending basket. A photograph of Michael Jordan taking the Shot was placed on the cover of the local telephone directory. The game-winning basket made Michael Jordan one of the best-known college basketball players in the country.

How did he celebrate? Only two days after winning the national championship, he was back in the gym, playing in pickup games, getting ready for his sophomore season.

At the end of the school year, James Worthy decided to leave college early and enter the NBA draft. Michael Jordan knew that in his sophomore year the Tar Heels would depend on him to make up for the loss of Worthy.

Michael spent hours in the gym every day. Although he was only playing in pickup games, the competition included many of his Tar Heel teammates and alumni from recent years. Michael's team usually won, and he would play for hours. He didn't leave the court until he was too exhausted to play anymore.

All the hard work paid off. Entering his sophomore season, Michael looked strong and powerful. He now stood six foot six. Everyone expected him to be the best player in college basketball.

But when the season began, the Tar Heels missed James Worthy. Although Michael was all over the court, stealing the ball, rebounding, and scoring almost at will, North Carolina didn't quite have the firepower of the year before. While they still managed to win the ACC championship, they lost to Georgia in the regionals of the NCAA tournament, 82–77. Michael scored 28 points in the losing effort, and the Tar Heels finished the 1982–83 season with a record of 28–8.

For the season, Michael had averaged exactly 20 points per game and was named the Tar Heels Defensive Player of the Game 12 times. At the end of the year, he was selected to virtually every All-American team and named Player of the Year by the *Sporting News*. But Michael wasn't satisfied; the loss to Georgia in the NCAA tournament hurt. He knew there was room for improvement in his game.

That summer, he was invited to join the United States basketball team playing in the Pan American games. Michael knew that playing against some of the best players in the world would help him improve his game and hone his skills. As a member of the team, he was able to travel to Caracas, Venezuela. The team won the gold medal, and visiting a foreign country opened Michael's eyes to a world outside the United States.

He became fascinated with different cultures. So, after talking with his academic adviser at the start of his junior year at North Carolina, he decided to become a geography major, specializing in cultural geography.

At the college level, geography is much more than just knowing the state capitals. It is a rigorous academic program that studies how landforms and other geographic features influence the development of societies. Michael enjoyed travel and thought the program would help him appreciate his experiences. He even hoped to become a geography teacher some day.

Michael took the academic side of college seriously. He had to. Every time he called home, the first thing his mother asked him about was his studies. Only after Michael assured her that he was studying hard and keeping up with his classwork would she ask him about basketball.

Yet it seemed unlikely that Michael would ever become a geography teacher. Entering his junior year, he was the best-known player in college basketball. Most people assumed that Michael Jordan's future would be in professional basketball. But for now, everyone expected him to lead the Tar Heels to another NCAA championship.

Coach Smith acknowledged that Michael had earned his place as team leader by giving him more responsibility. On defense, he was allowed to exercise his own judgment and leave his man if he thought he could make a steal or block a shot. In all his years of coaching, Coach Smith had only given two other players the same freedom.

But was Michael ready to take on so much so quickly? While North Carolina began the season with a string of victories, Michael played poorly. He suffered through the first shooting slump of his college career. Instead of scoring his usual 20 or 25 points per game, Michael struggled for every basket.

Everyone wondered what was wrong. Was Michael feeling the pressure? Was he becoming lazy? Did the constant double-team he faced from the opposition bother him? Was he really as good as people thought?

Michael asked himself the same questions. When he could not find an answer, he went to his father and asked for his advice.

"Son," James Jordan said, "you're trying to force things. You've got enough talent that if you just play like Michael Jordan, things will fall into place."

The advice soon worked. Michael started relaxing on the court and let the game come to him.

The Player of the Year was back. On January 29, the Tar Heels were losing to Louisiana State University at the end of the first half, 37–34. Then Michael Jordan took over the game.

In the final 20 minutes of play, Michael was everywhere, blocking shots, making steals, rebounding, and scoring baskets in increasingly spectacular fashion. He finished with 29 points, and North Carolina won in a rout, 90–79.

As Michael got better and better, the Tar Heels cruised through the remainder of the regular season. North Carolina easily won the ACC championship and tournament, finishing with a record of

27 wins and only 2 losses. Entering the NCAA tournament, the Tar Heels were ranked number one in the country.

In their first game, they easily defeated Temple University, 77–66. Michael was magnificent, hitting 11 of 15 shots and scoring 27 points.

The victory earned the Tar Heels the right to play Indiana University. Indiana Hoosiers coach Bobby Knight was considered one of the best college coaches in the nation, and his team reflected his basketball savvy. On offense, the Hoosiers were patient and disciplined. On defense, they controlled the tempo of the game and challenged every shot.

That style bothered North Carolina. The Tar Heels never got untracked, and for the first time in months, Michael had an off game, scoring only 13 points. North Carolina lost, 72–68.

Despite the loss, Michael collected a number of individual honors. Once again, he was named college basketball's Player of the Year and selected to virtually every All-American team. The pressure of the basketball season was over, but there was no rest for Michael Jordan. He had to make several important decisions.

After playing for three years at North Carolina, there was little left for Michael to accomplish in college basketball. His team had won an NCAA championship and three ACC championships. He himself had won almost every individual award college basketball offered. Over the last half of his third season, it became clear that the college game provided no challenge for his skills.

Michael Jordan was in the perfect position to enter professional basketball. In everyone's estimation, he ranked with the best three or four players in college basketball and was certain to be one of the first players selected in the NBA draft. He was also healthy. If he played another year of college basketball, Michael could get hurt. Even a minor injury in a college game could affect his chances to make it in the NBA.

Then there was the money. Michael knew that if he turned pro, he and his family would be wealthy beyond their wildest dreams. Michael's parents had worked hard their entire lives. Michael wanted to provide them with things they had done without in order to raise their children. Michael promised his mother a new house and he wanted to buy his father a car. He wanted both his parents to be able to retire.

But Michael's parents, particularly his mother, didn't care about the money he would make in professional basketball and the things he promised to buy. His mother's only dream was for Michael to receive his college degree. "No matter where you go and how much money you make," she told him, "you'll always have your education."

While Michael tried to decide whether or not to turn professional, he faced yet another challenge. He was invited to try out for the 1984 United States Olympic basketball team.

Unlike today, in 1984, professional players were not allowed to play for the United States Olympic team. The squad team was to be made up entirely of college players. So, in mid-April, 72 athletes were invited to try out for the team. Indiana coach Bobby Knight served as coach.

Many people thought that Michael Jordan would

have a hard time playing in Coach Knight's structured offense. Yet once the tryouts began, it was obvious to everyone, even Coach Knight, that Michael was a special player. Michael was spectacular on both ends of the court. To no one's surprise, Knight selected him for the Olympic team.

Playing for the Olympic team was an honor, but it didn't change the fact that Michael had a decision to make. The NBA draft took place before the Olympics. If Michael wanted to play professionally next season, he had to make up his mind — soon.

He went to talk with Coach Smith. Jordan respected the coach and knew Smith would be honest with him.

"Coach," asked Michael, "what do you think? Should I turn pro?"

As much as Smith enjoyed having Michael Jordan on his team, he was also a realist. He knew his star player was ready for the NBA. Smith didn't think it made any sense for Michael to take a chance playing another year of college basketball when some NBA team was willing to pay him millions of dollars.

Besides, Smith knew Michael Jordan's game was made for professional basketball. In college, Michael had to play within the confines of Smith's system. Smith knew that Michael often had to slow down in order to involve his teammates in the Tar Heel offense. The slashing drives and magnificent dunks that he made only once or twice a game at North Carolina would become commonplace in the NBA. Smith advised Michael to turn pro.

The deadline for making his decision was May 5. Until the very last moment, Michael was unsure what to do. On the evening of May 4, he went out to dinner with Buzz Peterson and kept asking his friend, "What should I do?"

Over and over again, Peterson replied, "I can't help you. You're the only person that knows the right answer."

The roommates talked late into the night, lying on their beds in their dorm room and staring at the ceiling. When Michael woke the next morning, he quietly got dressed and left for the press conference held for him to announce his decision.

By the time Michael arrived at the press conference, he had decided what to do. Although he knew how much his mother wanted him to get his degree, he had decided to turn pro. He promised his mother

41

that he wouldn't let professional basketball stop him from finishing his studies some day.

Michael looked around at the reporters and TV cameras, took a deep breath, and said, "I have to do what's best for me. If I owe anyone, it's my parents, who have put up with me for twenty years. Money plays a big part in our lives, but who knows? I may not be around next year. I think it's better to start now. But this wasn't solely a financial decision. Here was a chance to move up to a higher level."

College was over. Soon, Michael Jordan wouldn't be playing basketball just for fun anymore. Soon, it would be a full-time job. Basketball had become his life.

Chapter Three:
1984-1985

Rookie of the Year

Although Michael had made the decision to turn pro, his immediate future was uncertain. He still had to go through the NBA draft, then play for the Olympic team in Los Angeles.

While many people thought Michael would be successful in professional basketball, not everyone was as confident as Coach Smith. Some pro scouts thought Michael might have trouble making the transition from the college game. They wondered if his jump shot was accurate enough for him to play guard and if, at six foot six, he might be too small to play forward. While Michael had been the best player in college basketball, few thought he would become the best professional player.

The NBA draft was held on June 19, 1984. The Houston Rockets had the first pick. As expected, they selected University of Houston center Hakeem Olajuwon, the best pivot man in college basketball. The Rockets needed a center and selecting a player from the University of Houston was a smart public relations move.

The Portland Trail Blazers picked next. Many people thought Portland would pick Michael. But the Trail Blazers needed a center, too. They selected Sam Bowie of the University of Kentucky.

As soon as Portland made its pick, officials from the Chicago Bulls let out a big sigh of relief. The Bulls, with the third pick in the draft, had hoped that Michael Jordan would still be available.

In a Chicago hotel, thousands of Bulls fans watching the draft on television started chanting, "Jordan, Jordan, Jordan." Bulls general manager Rod Thorn, in a room two floors above the ballroom, could hear the commotion. A big smile crossed his face. A few moments later, the Bulls released a brief statement. "The Chicago Bulls Pick Michael Jordan, Guard, from the University of North Carolina."

As soon as the Bulls fans heard the announcement, they erupted in applause and cheers.

Ever since the Bulls franchise was born in 1966,

Bulls fans had been waiting for a winner. In the early 1970s, they nearly got their wish. The Bulls made regular appearances in the playoffs, and even won the Central Division championship in the 1971–72 season. But the team never went very far in the playoffs, and in the last decade had been doormats in the NBA. While the Bulls players were individually talented, they didn't play together well as a team. They didn't just lose; they lost badly. None of the Bulls demonstrated much leadership on court, and no one was particularly exciting to watch.

The Bulls hoped Michael Jordan would change all that. Members of the press started referring to him as the team's "savior." But before Michael could join the Bulls, he had some unfinished business to take care of. He still had to play in the Olympics.

All summer long, Michael practiced with the Olympic team. During a series of exhibitions, it became clear that even on a team that included stars like Georgetown's Patrick Ewing and St. John's guard Chris Mullin, Michael Jordan was the best player. In practice, even Coach Bobby Knight, who was known for his stern and serious disposition, marveled at Michael's ability. While Knight expected players to listen and do things his way on the court, he allowed Michael more freedom than others. Knight knew that once Michael got going, few players could stop him.

The world found out about Michael Jordan when the 1984 Olympics began in July.

In the first game, against China, Michael scored 14 points and led the United States to a lopsided win, 91–47. In the next game, versus Canada, he scored 20 as the United States won big again, 89–68. Then, in a 104–68 blasting of Uruguay, he dropped in 16 points as the United States moved on to the medal round.

Players from the opposing teams were awed by Michael Jordan. Many had never seen a player do the things he did. When he jumped into the air, he seemed to soar and "hang," as if defying gravity. He didn't just score; he did so in spectacular fashion, spinning 360 degrees then jamming the ball, or launching himself into the air from the free throw line and throwing down a tomahawk slam, or twisting beneath the basket for a reverse layup. As Uruguayan coach Ramon Etchamendi said about playing the American squad. "Maybe we have a chance with seven against five." One Canadian player lamented, "We just couldn't stay with Jordan."

Michael saved his best performances for medal-round play. In a 101–68 rout of Spain, he scored 24 points, 18 in the first half. After the game, Spanish coach Antonio Díaz-Miguel joked, "I asked my good friend Bob Knight if he wanted my whole team in trade for Michael Jordan."

To win the gold medal, the United States had to beat Spain for a second time. Coach Knight worried that his team would be overconfident. A U.S. Olympic victory was anything but a sure thing. Only four years before, in the 1980 Olympics, the United States had finished a disappointing third.

When Knight entered the locker room before the final game, he wondered what he could say to his team to get them ready. As he approached the black-board to write down his starting lineup, he noticed a note taped to the board. Knight looked at the note closely. It was from Michael Jordan.

"Coach," it read, "after everything we've been through, we're not going to lose this game."

The note was prophetic. Far from suffering from

a letdown or overconfidence, the team rode roughshod over Spain. Michael scored 20 points, and the United States knocked off Spain, 96–65, to win the gold.

After the medal ceremony, Michael found his mother, Deloris, in the crowd. Without saying a word, he took the gold medal from his neck and draped it around hers.

On a team of stars, Michael shone brightest, as he led the U.S. squad with a scoring average of 17 points. In eight games, the United States won by an average of 32 points.

Michael had little time to celebrate his Olympic accomplishments. As soon as the games ended, he signed a seven-year contract with the Chicago Bulls worth more than $6 million and began his professional career.

Coach Smith had been right. Professional basketball was perfectly suited to Michael's game. Each team had to play man-to-man defense, giving Michael more room to maneuver than he had had in college. The 24-second clock made the entire game move faster. Individual ability was highlighted, and few players had as much individual ability as Michael Jordan. The spectacular plays he made once or twice a game in college were commonplace in the NBA.

Even in practice, Bulls coach Kevin Loughery could tell Michael was going to be something special. As he told one reporter, when the Bulls scrimmaged, "If I put him in with the starters, they win. If I put him in with the second team, they win. . . . No matter what I do with Michael, his team wins."

In early October, Michael Jordan made his professional debut in an exhibition game against the Milwaukee Bucks played at a high school in East Chicago. While teenage girls screamed his name as if he were a rock star, Michael scored 22 points despite being guarded by Sidney Moncrief, the NBA Defensive Player of the Year! The Bulls won easily.

With each game, Michael played better and better. And he played just as hard in practice as he did during the games. Some Bulls players were accustomed to "coasting" through practice. But when Michael was on the floor, they soon began playing hard. If they didn't, Michael would easily embarrass them with his magnificent play.

When the regular season began, Michael barely

slowed down. It took him only a few games to adjust to the pace of the NBA. The Bulls won their opener, 109–93, against the Washington Bullets. Michael chipped in 16 points. In their second game, the Bulls lost to the Milwaukee Bucks, 108–106, when Michael missed a last-second shot. Two nights later, again against the Bucks, Michael broke out for 37 points as the Bulls won again.

Word of Michael Jordan traveled quickly through the league. Nearly every night, he dominated highlight programs shown on television. In every game he played, it seemed, Michael Jordan did something no one had ever seen before.

Almost overnight, Michael became the biggest drawing card in the NBA. No matter where he went, fans crowded around him and clamored after his autograph. After only a few weeks as a professional basketball player, Michael found it impossible to go to a movie or walk through a mall like a regular person. He was just too popular.

All over the country, young basketball players who had always imitated stars like Magic Johnson of the Los Angeles Lakers or Larry Bird of the Boston Celtics suddenly started imitating Michael Jordan.

On playgrounds everywhere, you could find kids driving to the hoop with their tongues sticking out like Michael. His Bulls jersey, number 23, became the most popular uniform, and his sneakers, known as Air Jordans, soon outsold all others.

Had this happened to any other player, it might have changed the way he or she behaved toward people. But Michael knew who he was. He knew that no matter how well he played basketball, what really mattered was how good a person he was. Just because he was the most popular player in the league didn't mean he could stop trying to improve or start treating people badly. His parents had taught him better than that.

While the Bulls weren't the best team in the league, they weren't the worst, either. With Michael leading the way, they finished the first half of the season 20–21.

In midseason, Michael was thrilled to learn he had been named to the NBA All-Star team. That had been one of his personal goals when he entered his first professional season.

But Michael was disappointed in the All-Star game. He played 22 minutes but took only nine shots. It seemed as if each time he was open, his teammates passed the ball the other way. When he did get the ball, the defense swarmed over him, and no one on his team came over to help out. After the game, Michael was mystified.

He soon found out what had happened. Some of the older players on Michael's team were jealous of all the attention he was receiving. Before the game, they decided to "freeze him out" — not let him have the ball.

When Michael Jordan found out what had happened, he didn't get mad; he got even. A few days after the All-Star game, the Bulls played the Detroit Pistons. Michael had learned that Piston guard Isiah Thomas was one of the players behind the All-Star game boycott.

Michael made him pay. He scored 49 points on a series of monster dunks, spinning drives, and soaring jump shots that left the Pistons shaking their heads. The Bulls won big.

Michael finished his first NBA season with a scoring average of 28.2 points a game. He also averaged 5.9 assists and 6.5 rebounds per game, remarkable numbers for any player. To no one's surprise, Michael Jordan was named NBA Rookie of the Year.

Thanks to Michael, the Bulls had become one of the most popular teams in the league. Attendance at Chicago Stadium had nearly doubled, and they were favorites on the road, too. Moreover, the Bulls improved their record to 38–44, good enough to make the playoffs.

Yet what happened on the basketball court was not the most important event in Michael Jordan's life that year. In midseason, Michael met Juanita Vanoy, a former model who was working as a secretary at an advertising agency that handled some of Michael's endorsements. Soon, Michael and Juanita were spending all their free time together. A few years later, they married.

All the way around, it had been an eventful season for Michael Jordan. But even he couldn't quite win games all by himself. The veteran Milwaukee Bucks bounced the Bulls from the playoffs in the first round, three games to one. Michael Jordan was disappointed but tried to put the loss behind him. He was already thinking about next year.

Chapter Four:
1985-1987

Getting "Bull"-ish on the Court

In the off-season, partly because of the success the team had had with Michael, the Bulls were sold to a group headed by Jerry Reinsdorf, who also owned the Chicago White Sox baseball team. The Bulls fired coach Kevin Loughery and general manager Rod Thorn and named Stan Albeck and Jerry Krauss to take their places. The two men made some off-season changes in the team. They got rid of several players who gave less than their full effort on the court, then added power forward Charles Oakley in the draft and moved forward Sydney Green into the starting lineup.

Entering the 1985–86 season, Michael was optimistic. He hoped to lead the Bulls to a winning record and a good performance in the playoffs.

But the Bulls had some problems that even

Dan Sears/Wilmington Morning Star

Michael Jordan plays on his high school team, the Laney Buccaneers. He wears number 23, the same number he would wear later as a member of the University of North Carolina Tar Heels and the Chicago Bulls.

A star player for the North Carolina Tar Heels, Number 23 makes his move!

Michael Jordan hangs from the hoop after a tremendous slam dunk.

Michael poses with the 1989 "Top Vote Getter" award just before the NBA All-Star game. He received more than one million votes!

Air Jordan flies again!

An emotional Michael Jordan cradles the 1991 NBA championship trophy.

Jordan aims, shoots, and scores the winning basket to give the Bulls their third straight NBA title in 1998.

Jordan, the series MVP, jumps in celebration after his 1998 title-winning shot drops through the hoop.

It's a whole new ballgame: Jordan, wearing his new Washington
Wizards uniform, waves to the crowd in Chicago.

The newest Wizard works his magic in a game against the Phoenix Suns.

Michael Jordan's Year-to-Year NBA Statistics

	Team	Games	Rebounds	Assists	Steals	Blocks	Points	Season Average
1984-85	Chicago	82	534	481	196	69	2,312	28.2
1985-86	Chicago	18	64	53	37	21	408	22.7
1986-87	Chicago	82	430	377	236	125	3,041	37.1
1987-88	Chicago	82	449	485	259	131	2,868	35.0
1988-89	Chicago	81	652	650	234	65	2,633	32.5
1989-90	Chicago	82	565	519	227	54	2,753	33.6
1990-91	Chicago	82	492	453	223	83	2,580	31.5
1991-92	Chicago	80	511	489	182	75	2,404	30.1
1992-93	Chicago	78	522	428	221	61	2,541	32.6
1993-94	------------------------------- Retired -------------------------------							
1994-95	Chicago	17	117	90	30	13	457	26.9
1995-96	Chicago	82	543	352	180	42	2,491	30.4
1996-97	Chicago	82	482	352	140	44	2,431	29.6
1997-98	Chicago	82	475	283	141	45	2,357	28.7
1998-2001	------------------------------- Retired -------------------------------							
2001-02	Washington	60	339	310	85	26	1,375	22.9
2002-03	Washington	82	497	311	123	39	1,640	20.0
TOTAL		1,072	6,672	5,633	2,514	893	32,292	

Michael Jordan's Career Highlights

1982:
Member of the NCAA champion North Carolina Tar Heels

1984:
College Player of the Year
Olympic gold medalist

1985:
NBA Rookie of the Year

1986:
Record for most points scored in an NBA playoff game (63)

1988:
Regular season MVP

1991:
Regular season MVP
Playoff MVP

1992:
Regular season MVP
Playoff MVP
Olympic gold medalist

1993:
Playoff MVP

1995-96:
Regular season MVP
Member of NBA Championship team
NBA Finals Most Valuable Player
NBA All-Defensive First Team

1996-97:
NBA Finals Most Valuable Player
Member of NBA Championship team
NBA All-Defensive First Team
All-NBA First Team

1997-98:
NBA Finals Most Valuable Player
Member of NBA Championship team
NBA All-Defensive First Team

2001-02:
Came out of retirement to play for Washington Wizards

Michael Jordan couldn't take care of. The team had a difficult time adjusting to a new coach, and some Bulls players were more interested in partying than they were in winning.

The team started off the exhibition season with eight straight losses. Then Quintin Dailey, who teamed with Michael in the Bulls' backcourt, asked to be sent to a drug rehabilitation program. Soon after, Michael's best friend on the team, Michael Higgins, was cut.

Despite all the changes and their poor exhibition season, the Bulls won their season opener against Cleveland, 116–115. Michael scored 29 points, including 7 in overtime.

The next night, the Detroit Pistons came to town. Late in the game, Michael drove to the basket. Detroit center Bill Laimbeer, known for his aggressive play, moved over to try to block Michael's shot.

Laimbeer missed the ball, but he didn't miss Michael, slamming him to the court. Michael's teammates rushed onto the floor, and the game was stopped for several minutes before the referees could restore order.

Once again, Michael got even. For the rest of the

quarter, he couldn't be stopped. He finished with 33 points, and the Bulls won again, 121–118.

Despite all their problems and changes, the Bulls were somehow 2–0. Maybe Michael was right to be optimistic.

On October 29, the Bulls traveled to Oakland, California, to play the Golden State Warriors. The Oakland Coliseum was packed with fans anxious to see Michael Jordan. When the game got going, he did not disappoint.

In the second period, Michael made a move to the basket. Suddenly, he fell to the floor. When he stood up, he couldn't put any weight on his left foot. His teammates had to help him to the locker room.

Michael missed the rest of the game, but the Bulls held on to win their third game in a row. Michael showed up at practice the next day on crutches. The team doctor diagnosed the injury as a sprained ankle.

But the pain in Michael's foot wouldn't go away. A week later, a CAT scan revealed a small break, and doctors placed the foot in a cast. They told Michael he would miss a couple months of the season.

Without Michael Jordan, the Bulls were not a very good basketball team. They lost four games in a row and were suddenly just as bad as they had been two seasons before.

The injury was slow to heal. As the Bulls dropped lower in the standings, Michael became frustrated and depressed. Coach Albeck and Jerry Krauss wanted him to travel with the team while he recovered, but Michael refused. He thought the team might play better if the players weren't always looking over their shoulders at him, wondering when he would return. "They need to have their own identity," he told reporters.

Unable to play, Michael decided it was time to make good on his promise to his mother. So instead of sitting around waiting for his ankle to heal, he went back to North Carolina and finished his degree.

Michael was finally able to return to action on March 15, 1986. He had missed a total of 64 games.

Bulls owner Jerry Reinsdorf wanted Michael to work his way back slowly, playing only a limited number of minutes in each game over the last few weeks of the season. He didn't want to risk another injury. But Michael wanted to play, and play hard. He couldn't stand to play any other way. Besides, despite their poor record, the Bulls still had an outside chance to make the playoffs.

It took Michael Jordan several weeks, and several long arguments with Reinsdorf, to finally get his way. But it didn't take him long to get the hang of basketball again. After being inserted into the lineup in the second quarter of a game against the Milwaukee Bucks, he took the ball straight to the hoop as soon as he touched it, dunking over seven-foot-three-inch Randy Breuer. As soon as Michael started playing full-time again, the Bulls started winning. By the end of the season, they had clinched the last spot in the playoffs.

Their first opponents in the playoffs were the great Boston Celtics, champions of the Eastern Conference and perhaps the best defensive team in the league. The Celtics were led by forward Larry Bird, the smartest and arguably the best player in the NBA. Celtic guard Dennis Johnson, considered one of the league's top defensive guards, would be guarding Michael. No one gave the Bulls a chance.

But after sitting out for much of the season, Michael was well rested. His foot was completely healed, and he was at the peak of his game. The Celtics paid the price.

In game one, played in Boston, Michael started out by hitting his first five shots. The Celtics double-teamed him every time he had the ball. That hardly slowed him down.

He scored over, under, and around every Celtic player who tried to guard him. He hit for an amazing 49 points — nearly half the Bulls' total score. But after trailing by only two at halftime, the Bulls eventually lost, 123–104.

In game two, Michael was even better. He moved through the Celtics as though their sneakers were filled with concrete. If he was challenged out front, he slashed to the basket and jammed the ball. If a player tried to block his shot, he soared around him and laid in a reverse finger roll. When the defense backed off, Michael calmly canned a jumper. There was simply no way to stop him, and toward the end of the fourth quarter, he made it clear he was out to win.

With only seconds remaining and the Bulls down

by two points, Michael launched a three-pointer. The ball rolled off the rim, but he was fouled on the shot. He sank both free throws to tie the game and send it into overtime.

The Bulls let Michael work his magic. He and the Celtics traded baskets in the extra period. It was five-on-one and Michael was holding his own. At the end of overtime, the score was tied again.

In the second overtime, the Celtics finally pulled ahead and won, 135–131. But Michael had scored an unbelievable 63 points. No one in NBA history had ever scored that many points during a playoff game.

Even though they had won, after the game, the Celtics could only talk about Michael Jordan. Celtic captain Larry Bird was most effusive in his praise. "I could't believe anybody could do that against the Boston Celtics," Bird told reporters. "It shows you what kind of person he is. I think he's God disguised as Michael Jordan."

The Bulls and Celtics traveled to Chicago for game three. Despite the fact that he had home-court advantage, Michael Jordan couldn't maintain his intensity. After his remarkable performance in games one and two, he scored only 19 points with 10 assists and 9 rebounds before fouling out with five minutes remaining. The Bulls lost, 122–104. The season was over, but one thing was clear — Michael Jordan was the most exciting player in the NBA.

Michael was doing things that no single basketball player had ever done before. It was as if the greatest players of all time had been combined into one person. His old hero David Thompson had always been considered the greatest leaper in the NBA, but Michael jumped just as well as Thompson. When Michael jumped, he seemed to hang in the air. Defenders went up with him, but they fell back to earth while he was still rising. Julius Erving of the Philadelphia 76ers had been considered the best dunker in the NBA, but not even Doctor J could do some of the 360-degree reverse slam jams Michael was now making. Magic Johnson of the Los Angeles Lakers and Larry Bird of the Celtics were considered the most complete players in the game, but now some people were saying that Michael could pass the ball, rebound, and defend as well as either man.

But Michael was not satisfied with his personal accomplishments. As much as he liked to score, he liked to win even more. He wouldn't be satisfied until the Bulls were winners.

That summer the team had another new coach. Doug Collins stepped in and replaced Stan Albeck. Like his predecessor, Collins turned Michael Jordan loose.

When the 1986–87 season began, Michael picked up right where he had left off. In the exhibition season, he scored over 40 points nine times. Four times he scored over 50 points, and in one game he scored 61. Not since seven-foot center Wilt Chamberlain averaged 50.4 points per game in the 1961–62 season had any NBA player scored so many points.

Michael kept right on going in the regular season. With virtually the same lineup as the year before, the Bulls needed him to score as much as possible to have a chance to win. No one else on the team was as consistent a scorer.

Every time the Bulls stepped onto the court in

1986–87, the game featured a solo performance by Michael Jordan. Somehow, he seemed to keep getting better. Over the course of the season, he scored more than 30 points an amazing 62 times. In 36 of those games, he scored over 40 points; six times he broke the 50-point mark; and twice he hit over 60 points.

Opposing teams were helpless to stop him. Neither double-teams nor triple-teams made much of a difference. Michael often saved his best for late in the game, as if he relished the pressure. Several times during the season, he outscored the other team in the final quarter. In one game, against the New York Knicks, he scored the Bulls' last eighteen points to help Chicago win by two, 101–99.

Michael cemented his status as the most exciting player in the NBA during the All-Star weekend at the Kingdome in Seattle, Washington. He participated in the slam-dunk contest and came away with his first slam-dunk title. He called his winning dunk the "Kiss the Rim" jam. The victory earned Michael $12,000, which he split among his Bull teammates.

Yet Michael was more than a scoring machine and

human highlight film. He did whatever he could to help his team. When Bulls coach Doug Collins asked Michael to play forward sometimes so he could put another shooter into the guard spot, Michael readily agreed. In addition to averaging 37.1 points per game — third best in NBA history — Michael also averaged five rebounds and nearly five assists. His total of 236 steals was second best in the league, and his 125 blocked shots led the Bulls.

Still, when playoff time rolled around, it was the same old story. The Bulls played the Celtics again. Michael was magnificent, but Boston won in three games.

Some sportswriters around the league took delight in the Bulls' defeat. They thought Michael Jordan, despite his obvious ability, was a selfish player. They referred to the Bulls as "Team Jordan," as if the other players just didn't matter.

Michael Jordan had accomplished nearly everything possible on the basketball court. Although he had collected both an NCAA title and an Olympic gold medal, one goal still eluded him: an NBA championship. Michael knew that until his team won a championship, there would still be some critics who thought of him as something less than a complete player.

And good as he was, not even Michael Jordan could win an NBA championship all by himself.

Chapter Five:
1987–1990

"There's Michael Jordan and Then Everybody Else."

If Michael Jordan was ever to reach his goal of winning the NBA championship, he needed some help. The Bulls needed better players and someone else who could score. Center Dave Corzine, a former All-Star, was near the end of his career and soon would have to be replaced. Apart from Michael, Charles Oakley was the only Bulls player who was much of a scoring threat, and most of his points came on rebounds. Guard John Paxson was a good outside shooter, but he was unable to create his own shot. In short, there was no one to pick up the scoring slack if Michael slipped below his usual standards.

Moreover, the Bulls needed help on defense. Even when Michael Jordan did score 40 or 50 points, the Bulls sometimes lost. They couldn't keep the other team from scoring. The Bulls just weren't good enough to challenge for the NBA title.

Before the 1987–88 season, the Bulls finally got a little help. In the NBA draft, the Bulls selected forwards Scottie Pippen and Horace Grant. Grant was a big banger who could rebound, play defense, and post up under the basket. Pippen was more of a finesse player. Quick and aggressive on defense, Pippen always looked for the steal and was willing to dive after loose balls. On offense, he could run the floor and hit the jump shot.

When the Bulls opened the season, Michael worked to prove his critics wrong. Now that he had a surrounding cast, he became more of a playmaker, passing the ball, setting picks, and sometimes acting as a decoy.

The strategy worked. The Bulls jumped off to a 7–1 start. On occasion, Michael was as explosive as ever, hitting for 40 or more points in a game. But he was content to score much less if the Bulls could still win.

Keyed by the addition of Pippen and Grant, the Bulls surprised everyone and finished the first half of the 1987–88 season 27–18. When the NBA elite gathered in Chicago for the All-Star weekend, the Bulls were the talk of the league.

The Bulls' impressive first-half performance gave Michael added stature in the eyes of his peers at the All-Star game. For the first time, they accorded him the respect his talent deserved.

Michael easily won the slam-dunk competition, and during the game the next day, his All-Star teammates deferred to him in front of his hometown crowd, feeding him the ball time after time. Michael responded with a spectacular day, hitting 17 of 23 shots, finishing with 40 points — only two short of the All-Star game record — and being named Most Valuable Player (MVP).

After the game, a reporter asked Magic Johnson how he ranked the best players in the league. Johnson looked at the reporter and smiled. "There's Michael Jordan," he said, "and then everybody else."

Yet in the second half of the season, the Bulls started to struggle. Their younger players, particularly rookies Grant and Pippen, hit "the wall," a slump that most players face in their first NBA season. For a while, it was "Team Jordan" again.

Then the Bulls traded for Seattle guard Sam

Vincent. Vincent gave Chicago a true point guard and some additional firepower. He sparked the club, Pippen and Grant got their second wind, and the Bulls roared to the finish line, winning 17 of their last 23 games to end the season 50–32. They were tied for second in the Central Division, only four games behind first-place Detroit. While the Bulls were still long shots to win the championship, for the first time since Michael Jordan had joined the team, they entered the playoffs expecting to succeed.

The Bulls played Cleveland in the first round. Chicago was favored to win the best-of-five series.

But many of the younger Bulls had never been in the playoffs before. When the first game started, they were nearly frozen with fear.

Michael did not want to lose. In the regular season, he had often waited for his teammates to come back down to earth. But this was the playoffs. He couldn't afford to wait.

Michael Jordan took over. In game one, he scored 50 of the Bulls' 104 points in a 104–93 win. In the second quarter, he personally outscored Cleveland, 21–19.

In game two, he was even better. This time, he scored 55 points, and the Bulls won again, 106–101.

Yet even Michael Jordan couldn't score 50 points in every game. In game three, he scored "only" 28 points, and the Bulls lost, 110–102. In the fourth game, Michael hit for 40, but the Bulls lost again, 97–91.

Although Michael could win the occasional game by himself, he couldn't win the whole series. If the Bulls were going to advance in the playoffs, Michael Jordan needed the kind of help the younger players had provided in the regular season.

He finally got it. His young teammates settled down in game five. Shots that had rolled around the hoop and out finally started dropping in. Michael scored 39, but Scottie Pippen helped out with 24 points and some important steals. The Bulls won, 108–101, and earned the right to play the Detroit Pistons in the next round.

The Pistons had forged a well-deserved reputation as the roughest, toughest defensive team in the league. Nicknamed "the Bad Boys," they saw what Michael Jordan had done to Cleveland and set out to stop him. The Pistons thought that if they shut him down, none of the other Bulls could hurt them.

The Pistons installed a complex, special defense they called "the Jordan Rules." Throughout the series, All-Star guard Joe Dumars hounded Michael from one end of the court to the other. As soon as Michael got the ball, he was harassed by a second player who tried to block his way to the basket and cut down his passing lanes. If Michael did break free, center Bill Laimbeer, forward Dennis Rodman, and the Pistons' other big men knocked him to the floor.

Some of the younger Bulls were intimidated by Detroit's rough play. The Pistons slowed Michael down, and none of his teammates picked up the slack. The Bulls simply couldn't match Detroit's intensity, and the Pistons won the series in five games.

The Bulls' 1987–88 season was over. Michael again led the league in scoring, averaging 35 points per game and improving his shooting percentage from 48 percent to over 53 percent. But the championship ring he had hoped for was still missing from his finger.

Over the next two years, the Bulls' starting lineup grew considerably stronger. Veteran center Bill Cartwright joined the team, replacing the aging Corzine in the starting lineup, and both Scottie Pippen and Horace Grant were beginning to play like All-Stars.

Then, in 1989, the Bulls replaced coach Doug Collins with Phil Jackson. Jackson tinkered with the Bulls offense and installed a half-court game to complement the Bulls fast break. While it took the team most of the 1989–90 season to learn the new setup, the benefits were clear. Michael Jordan still led the league in scoring in both 1988–89 and 1989–90, but for the first time since he had joined the team, everyone in the starting lineup averaged in double figures. The Bulls were becoming more than a one-man team.

But nothing the Bulls did in the regular season made much of a difference when they reached the playoffs. Each year, they had to play the Pistons. The Bulls just couldn't figure out a way to beat Detroit.

Yet Chicago improved ever so slightly each year. The Pistons defeated the Bulls in four straight games in the 1988–89 playoffs, but in the 1989–90 matchup, Chicago pushed Detroit to a full seven games. Detroit won the NBA championship each time —but the Bulls were drawing closer.

Winning an NBA championship was important to Michael Jordan. That was all that separated him from Magic Johnson and Larry Bird. Observers had noted many times that while Michael was the best individual player in the game, he didn't seem to be the best *team* player. He knew that until the Bulls won a championship, he would always be criticized.

Out on the asphalt and concrete courts of public opinion, Michael was already the champion. He was easily the most popular player in the game, particularly with kids. From the glass-strewn outdoor courts of the inner city, to the polished wood surfaces of suburban high school gyms, to dirt-packed backyard courts like his own Rack, Michael Jordan was the most popular player of all time. Young and old, black and white, male and female, everyone with even a passing interest in basketball loved Michael Jordan.

Yet his widespread popularity was a double-edged sword. On the one hand, doing what he loved best made him wealthy beyond his wildest dreams. Michael Jordan basketball shoes, Air Jordans, are the best-selling sneakers of all time. His contract with Nike, the manufacturer, is worth over $20 million. In 1989, the Bulls renegotiated his contract and gave Michael an eight-year contract worth $25 million. At the time, it was the biggest contract in the history of professional basketball. The Bulls set a new attendance record nearly every season and they were the most popular team on the road. Michael formed his own corporations and employed his parents and other members of his family. He was able to build James and Deloris a new house and give them new cars. He contributed thousands of dollars to charities and met presidents and world-famous entertainers.

But as Michael Joradan became more and more famous, it became difficult for him to live like other people. When the Bulls arrived in a city, Michael had to check in to the hotel under an assumed name. Usually, the team even had to post a guard at his door to keep fans from breaking in. If he tried to leave his room to go shopping, he was mobbed by autograph-seeking fans. It was almost impossible for Michael to do the things the rest of us take for granted, like take a walk on a nice spring day, sit in a restaurant and eat a meal, or even go down to the park on the corner and shoot some hoops. He was just too popular.

All that attention might make people bigheaded. But not Michael Jordan. His old friends and family say that despite his fame and wealth, he is the same person. Whenever possible, he goes out of his way to help others. Michael is friendly with his teammates off the court. He doesn't act as if he's better than they are. And once in a while, Michael will sneak out of a hotel and duck into a fast-food restaurant for a quick bite, or walk onto the court at a busy city park and start talking with the kids, usually leaving them with his sneakers and jersey when he is through.

By the beginning of the 1990–91 season, basketball had helped Michael Jordan acquire just about everything a person could want: wealth, fame, a loving family, and the opportunity to do what he loved best for a living. Yet by the time the season started,

Chapter Six:
1990–1991

Champions!

The Bulls started the 1990–91 season losing three of their first four games. But they did not panic. This time, Michael Jordan's teammates didn't look to Air Jordan to shoot the team out of a slump by scoring 40 or 50 points. They simply went to work and started playing better basketball.

The Bulls defense was much improved. While everyone still considered the Pistons the best defensive team in the league, the Bulls were starting to earn a reputation of their own.

On Christmas Day, the Bulls and Pistons faced off in a nationally televised game many thought would be a preview of the playoffs.

The Bulls were ready to play from the opening whistle. After a close first half, Chicago slowly pulled away. They buckled down on defense. They challenged every shot, and when Detroit missed, the Bulls didn't let the Pistons get the rebound. The Detroit players were intimidated by the aggressive Bulls and shot only 26 percent in the second half, scoring only 36 points. Michael scored 37 in the game to lead the Bulls to a 98–86 win.

The victory set the tone for the remainder of the season. Chicago stormed through the league and finished with a record of 61–21, second best in the NBA and a franchise record. The Bulls won the Central Division, and the defending champion Pistons finished in second place, 11 games back.

Entering the playoffs, Michael Jordan was cautiously optimistic. "We're good enough to win it," he told a reporter. "We know we can beat the teams we're going to meet in the playoffs. My job is to take on the leadership role and take us to the next level."

In the first round, the Bulls faced the New York Knicks. Despite the presence of star center Patrick Ewing, the Knicks just couldn't keep up with Chicago. The Bulls won three straight and the right to play Philadelphia in the second round. Meanwhile, the Pistons beat Atlanta and also advanced.

The Philadelphia 76ers, led by All-Star forward Charles Barkley, matched up well against the Bulls. During the regular season, they had defeated Chicago in three out of four games.

But once the series began, the Bulls were unstoppable. They played almost perfect basketball, and Pippen and Grant both turned in nearly flawless performances. In game four, with the Bulls up two games to one, Scottie Pippen scored 20, Horace Grant hit for 22, and Michael Jordan chipped in a quiet 25. The Bulls won, 101–85. Then they dumped the 76ers in game five to take the series four games to one. After the final game, all anyone could talk about was how well the Bulls played together as a team.

Meanwhile, the Pistons defeated the Celtics in six games. Once again, Chicago would battle Detroit for the Eastern Conference championship. The winner would go to the finals. If the Bulls hoped to win the championship, they had to beat Detroit.

The Pistons weren't quite the same team that had

beaten the Bulls in the playoffs for three years in a row. They were getting older, and several players were hobbled by injuries. Still, there was a reason the Pistons were the defending champions. Isiah Thomas and Joe Dumars were two of the best guards in the league, and Dennis Rodman and Bill Laimbeer were fearless underneath the basket. Although the Bulls were narrow favorites, everyone expected the best-of-seven-game series to be a war.

Before game one, Michael reassured his younger teammates. "They're beatable," he told them. "We just have to find a way." The way to beat Detroit, the Bulls now knew, was through teamwork and defense.

Game one was a typical Chicago-Detroit matchup — rough, tough, and low scoring. After three periods, the Bulls led, 68–65.

In previous years, this was the time of the game when Detroit's defense had always taken control. They had swarmed over Michael Jordan and watched as the other Bulls made mistakes and committed turnovers, leading to easy baskets for the Pistons.

But this year was different. The Bulls were a different team. While the Pistons focused on Michael, a couple of Bull reserves, Craig Hodges and Cliff Levingston, keyed a fourth-quarter run that put the Bulls ahead to stay. Although Michael Jordan scored only 22 points in the game, the Bulls won, 94–83.

The big loss shattered Detroit's confidence. The Bulls defense was intimidating the Pistons, while the offense spread points up and down the lineup. Chicago swept Detroit in four games and earned the right to play the Los Angeles Lakers in the NBA Finals.

The Lakers, led by guard Magic Johnson, had won the NBA championship three times in the last decade and were known as the "Team of the 80s." Even though the 1980s were over, they were still a formidable opponent.

Magic Johnson rivaled Michael Jordan for the title of best player in the league. He deserved much of the credit for L.A.'s performance. The unselfish point guard made everyone on his team a better player and keyed L.A.'s vaunted fast break, known as "Showtime." He had plenty of help from teammates James Worthy and Sam Perkins, Michael Jordan's former teammates at North Carolina. The Lakers, with previous championship experience, were favored to win.

The finals opened in Chicago. In game one, the Lakers taught the Bulls a lesson and demonstrated why they were champions. Los Angeles out-thought and out-hustled the Bulls for a full 48 minutes.

Instead of running their fast break, the Lakers slowed down and played a patient half-court offense. The strategy shook up the Bulls and allowed the Lakers to control the pace of the game. The Bulls fast break never got on track. In the final seconds, Sam Perkins hit a three-pointer to put L.A. up by two, and when Michael Jordan's desperation 18-footer rattled out of the basket, L.A. escaped with a 93–91 win.

Michael took matters into his own hands in game two. But instead of turning the game into a demonstration of Team Jordan, he acted as playmaker. Throughout the first quarter, he passed up shots of his own to set up his teammates for easy baskets. By involving everyone in the game, he was able to disrupt the Lakers' slow-down strategy. At halftime, the Bulls led, 48–43.

By the third quarter, the Bulls offense was working on all cylinders. Michael Jordan had pulled a Magic Johnson and made everyone on the team better. The Lakers didn't know who to guard anymore. In the third quarter, the Bulls scored 38 points to turn the game into a rout. Michael Jordan even got into the act. Over the last part of the third quarter and the beginning of the fourth, he hit 13 straight shots in one of the most remarkable performances ever in the NBA Finals.

One play in particular left fans talking for days. Early in the fourth quarter, Michael took a pass on the break and charged down the lane to the hoop. As he rose for a shot, he lifted the ball high in the air with his right hand and appeared poised for a dunk.

But his old Tar Heel teammate Sam Perkins had other ideas. Perkins, who was six foot ten and had the longest arms in the league, moved in front of Michael. In perfect position, Perkins jumped up to swat the ball away.

His hand found only air. The ball was gone. When

Michael saw Perkins reach out, he calmly pulled the ball down, switched it to his left hand, then twisted under and around the shocked Perkins to flip in an underhand scoop shot off the glass. After the ball went in, Michael seemed surprised. He raced down the court with an "even-I-can't-believe-it" look on his face while the crowd went crazy. The Bulls roared to victory, 107–86, and tied the series at one game each.

The Bulls traveled to Los Angeles for game three. The Lakers made the most of their home-court advantage and carved out a comfortable lead. But near the end of the third quarter, the Bulls reserves keyed another big run. Chicago won going away, 104–96.

Game four was a given. Both James Worthy and Laker guard Byron Scott were injured, and the demoralized Lakers missed both players. L.A. never got untracked. Michael Jordan scored 28 points and dished out 13 assists. The Bulls won, 97–83, to take a commanding three-games-to-one lead in the series.

Still, the Lakers hadn't won three championships in the 1980s by giving up without a fight. In game five, before their home crowd, they played like champions. But the Bulls played better.

With a little more than six minutes left to play in the fourth quarter, L.A. nursed a three-point lead. Then the Bulls stepped up. First, Scottie Pippen hit a three-pointer to tie the game. Then, on the Bulls' next four possessions, John Paxson went unconscious, hitting three consecutive jumpers and a layup. All of a sudden, the Bulls led by ten.

Then Sam Perkins countered for the Lakers. He scored eight straight points to draw Los Angeles to within two points of the Bulls, 103–101.

In earlier seasons, with such a critical game on the line, the Bulls would have looked for Michael Jordan to take the ball one-on-one to the hoop. This year, the Bulls were a team.

As the clock ticked off the last seconds of the game, Michael got the ball. As soon as the Lakers started to collapse on him, he calmly fired a pass to a wide-open John Paxson. Paxson threw up a jump shot. The ball hit nothing but net. The Bulls led by four points. A few moments later, as a shocked L.A. audience looked on, the game ended. The Bulls had won, 108–101. They were champions of the NBA!

As soon as the buzzer sounded, Michael Jordan began embracing his teammates. Then they dashed through the fans beginning to swarm over the court and headed toward the locker room. When Michael reached the locker room, he was overcome with emotion. He collapsed to his knees and started to cry.

In a locker-room ceremony, NBA commissioner David Stern awarded the championship trophy to Bulls owner Jerry Reinsdorf. Reinsdorf held it for a moment, then passed the trophy to Michael. Michael sat in front of his locker, holding the trophy as gently as if it were a newborn baby, tears of joy running down his face. On one side of him sat his father, James Jordan. On the other side was his wife, Juanita.

"I never thought I'd be this emotional," he said to a television announcer, "but this is a great feeling."

"It was a seven-year struggle," he added. "When I first got to Chicago, we started at the bottom and every year worked harder and harder 'til we got to it. I've appreciated so much in my life from my family, from my kids, everything, but this is the most proud day I've ever had.

"Now we can get rid of the stigma of the one-man team. We did it as a team all season long."

Chapter Seven:
1991-1992

A Couple of Scars

Michael Jordan could at last add "NBA champion" to his list of outstanding accomplishments. But he still wasn't satisfied. He wanted to win another championship. He knew that to be considered a really great player, a team player like Magic Johnson or Larry Bird, he'd have to win more than one title.

Michael soon learned that winning a second championship would be harder than winning the first one. With a championship ring on his finger, he was under more scrutiny and more pressure than ever. Long before he had a chance to add another ring, Michael Jordan confronted a series of troubles unlike any he had ever faced.

The first problem surfaced in early October, just as the Bulls were ready to begin training camp. Like many other championship teams, the Bulls were invited to the White House to meet the president. Michael, who had already met President Bush, decided to skip the visit and spend the day with his family.

The press was shocked when Michael failed to turn up. Some writers wrote that his decision to spend the day with his family was an example of the way the Bulls gave Michael Jordan special treatment. Teammate Horace Grant made the same charges.

Michael defused the situation before it got out of control. He explained to the media that the Bulls knew he was going to miss the visit to the White House and had given him permission. Then, when training camp opened, he met with Horace Grant. The two players settled their differences. With the season ready to start, Michael wanted to make sure the Bulls focused fully on basketball.

For a while, they did. When the season opened, the Bulls played better than ever. In November, they ran off a franchise-record 14-game winning streak.

Then came the news that shocked and saddened

everyone in the NBA, including Michael. In a televised press conference, his friend Laker guard Magic Johnson announced that he was retiring from the NBA. He was infected with the HIV virus, which causes AIDS, and needed to concentrate on his health.

At the same time, Celtic forward Larry Bird was sidelined with a back injury and talking of retirement himself. The torch was being passed to Michael Jordan. He was now without question the best player in the game.

Throughout the 1991–92 season, he proved it was a title he deserved. By midseason, the Bulls were 37–5 and on pace to break the league record of 69 wins set by the Lakers in the 1971–72 season.

But the Bulls slumped in the second half. The pressure of being the defending NBA champs was getting to everyone. In February, at the end of a triple-overtime loss to Utah, a frustrated Michael even got into an argument with a referee and was suspended for a game.

Then Michael found himself in more serious trouble. A newspaper reported that the Bulls' star player had bet and lost thousands of dollars while playing golf and poker. In most states, gambling is illegal. Technically, Michael Jordan had broken the law. To make matters worse, some of the men he had gambled with had criminal records.

Professional sports are very sensitive to gambling. Teams don't want anyone to think that players aren't playing to win. While no one charged that Michael had bet on basketball, the revelations tarnished his image.

In a statement to the press, Michael explained: "At some point in my life, I was going to have to face this. Very few people go through their lifetimes without scars. I went through a six-, seven-year period without them. Now I have a couple of scars. The scars won't go away, but you know I'm going to be a better person because of them."

The NBA determined that Michael had broken no league rules but warned him to pay closer attention to who his friends were. In time, he was able to put the incident behind him.

The Bulls stormed through the remainder of the season and went on to win the Central Division, finishing 67–15, ten games ahead of second-place Cleveland. Once again, Michael Jordan led the league in scoring with an average of 30.1 points per game and was named league MVP for the third time.

The Bulls entered the playoffs knowing they faced their toughest challenge yet. While the Pistons, Lakers, and Celtics were not the tough teams they had once been, the New York Knicks, Cleveland Cavaliers, and Portland Trail Blazers were all much improved and had their sights set on an NBA title.

After defeating the Miami Heat in three straight games in the opening round, the Bulls were tested in round two against the Knicks. Like the Pistons a few years before, the Knicks were known as the roughest and toughest defensive team in the league. They gave the Bulls all they could handle. Entering game seven, the series was tied.

Michael Jordan led the way. In the first quarter, he exploded for 18 points, and the Bulls opened up a big lead. The Knicks never recovered. Michael finished with 42, and the Bulls won in a rout, 110–81. The Bulls were one step closer to their goal.

Next up were the Cleveland Cavaliers. A good team, the Cavs put up a monumental fight, but in the end, the Bulls dispatched them in six tough games to win the Eastern Conference. The Bulls moved on to face the Portland Trail Blazers in the finals.

Trail Blazer fans saw the series as a showdown between Michael Jordan and Portland star Clyde Drexler. Next to Michael, Drexler was probably the most exciting player in the league. While he wasn't quite as big as Michael, Portland fans thought that Drexler had a better jump shot and was more dangerous from the outside.

In the first game, in Chicago, Michael showed Trail Blazer fans who had a good outside shot. On his way to 35 first-half points, he made six of nine three-pointers, including a remarkable five in a row. The Bulls won big, 122–89.

But the Trail Blazers weren't finished. In game two, they fought back to tie the score at the end of regulation play, then snuck out of Chicago Stadium with a 115–104 win in overtime.

The two teams then traveled to Portland. The Bulls played great team defense and won by ten, holding the Trail Blazers to only 84 points. In game four, Portland bounced back again, however, and knotted the series at two games apiece.

Now the Bulls were the team with championship

experience. It showed. Instead of turning to Michael Jordan to do everything, Chicago clamped down on defense and made sure everyone was involved in the offense. They easily beat Portland, 112–89, in game five. The Bulls returned triumphantly to Chicago with a chance to win it all.

Bulls fans looked forward to seeing their team win an NBA championship on their home court. From the opening tip-off, they were on their feet cheering.

Portland hung close, but the Bulls would not be denied. When the final buzzer sounded, the scoreboard read HOME 97, VISITORS 93 . The Bulls were champions again!

The fans stood on their feet and cheered as Michael and his teammates danced with joy on the court at Chicago Stadium. Michael was again named playoff MVP and became the first player ever to win the MVP award in consecutive seasons for both the regular season and the playoffs.

"Come next June you'll probably be expecting a third from me," he told the media after the game, "but for now this championship proves the first one was no fluke." In reference to his earlier troubles, he then added: "This season has been a learning experience for me. I'm a better person for everything that has happened."

That was bad news for the other teams in the NBA. If there was anything they didn't need, it was for Michael Jordan to get any better than he already was.

Chapter Eight:
1992-1993

The "Dream Team" and Beyond

After such a grueling season, no one would have blamed Michael Jordan if he had taken the summer off. But he didn't. For the second time in his basketball career, he joined the United States Olympic basketball team.

In 1992, for the first time ever, professional athletes were allowed to compete in the Olympics. Playing with a team of collegians in 1988, the United States had lost to the Soviet Union. Determined to avenge the 1988 loss, they created a "Dream Team" made up of the best players in the NBA, plus one college player.

Magic Johnson came out of retirement to play on the team, and Larry Bird decided to join him. Utah forward Karl Malone and point guard John Stockton agreed to play, as did centers Patrick Ewing of the

Knicks and David Robinson of the Spurs, forward Chris Mullin of the Golden State Warriors, Clyde Drexler of the Trail Blazers, and Charles Barkley of the Phoenix Suns. Even Michael Jordan's teammate Scottie Pippen agreed to play. Christian Laettner of Duke represented the NCAA.

At first, Michael was unsure whether or not to play. He was tired, and he wanted to spend time with his family. Then Michael realized that the 1992 Olympics gave him a unique opportunity. He would have a chance to win a second Olympic gold medal, something very few athletes have been able to do. He would also have the chance to be a teammate of players like Bird and Magic. As opponents, each had pushed the others to play their very best. All-Star games gave them a chance to play together, but as Olympians, they'd all be reaching for the same goal.

Before the Olympics even began, the U.S. team had to qualify in a pre-Olympic tournament. In the very first game, Michael made the play of the tournament. As a ball bounced free at the sidelines near midcourt, he raced to save it. He leaped out of bounds, caught the ball, and fired a behind-the-back pass to a wide-open Larry Bird under the basket! Only then did he crash-land into the stands.

Despite the fact that Bird missed most of the tournament with a sore back and guard John Stockton broke a bone in his hand, the United States swept to five straight victories, winning by an average of more than 50 points. They were more than ready to face the best the world had to offer.

The Olympics were held in Barcelona, Spain, in late July and early August. From the moment the Dream Team arrived, its members were the most popular athletes at the Olympics. Off the court, athletes from all over the world swarmed the NBA stars at every opportunity. No one was more popular than Michael Jordan. The games were broadcast around the globe, soon making Michael Jordan the most recognizable athlete in the world.

On the court, the Dream Team was unstoppable. In most games, they opened up a huge early lead and spent much of the rest of the game entertaining the crowd with a dizzying variety of astounding plays. Sometimes, even their opponents just stopped and watched in amazement.

On the best team in the world, Michael Jordan

was the best player. Because the team had so much firepower, Michael spent most of the tournament passing the ball, rebounding, and playing defense. He helped make sure everyone was involved in the offense.

The Dream Team won all eight games it played, crushing Croatia 117–85 in the finals to win the gold medal. In that game, Michael led the United States in scoring, going 10–16 from the field to finish with 21 points. For the second time in as many tries, a gold medal hung around Michael Jordan's neck.

As satisfying as that accomplishment was, when the Olympics were over, both Michael Jordan and Scottie Pippen were exhausted. They had gone right from the NBA Finals straight to the Olympics, so it seemed as if their basketball season had never ended. Now, only a few weeks after the Olympics, it was time to begin working toward another NBA championship.

Everyone was wondering whether or not Michael Jordan and the Bulls could "three-peat" — win the championship for the third time in a row. Not even Magic Johnson's Lakers or Larry Bird's Celtics had been able to accomplish that. In fact, no NBA team except for the Boston Celtics of the 1960s, who won 11 titles in 13 years, and the Minneapolis Lakers of the 1950s had ever won three titles in a row.

Early in the 1992–93 season, it didn't look as if the Bulls had much of a chance. They got off to a slow start and in January actually lost more games than they won. The Phoenix Suns and the New York Knicks were both much improved and were playing better than the Bulls. Michael Jordan and Scottie Pippen were tired, Bill Cartwright's knees were bothering him, and John Paxson was sidelined with an injury.

But the team got its second wind in the second half of the season. The Bulls started running again and closed with a rush, winning the Central Division with a 57–25 record, third best in the league behind Phoenix and New York. Michael himself finished with a flourish and won his seventh consecutive scoring title with a 32.6 average.

The Bulls started the playoffs playing as if they didn't know how to lose. They beat the Atlanta Hawks and the Cleveland Cavaliers in rounds one and two without a defeat. Then the Bulls ran into a stone wall: the New York Knicks.

The Knicks' tough defense slowed the Bulls' fast-breaking offense. New York center Patrick Ewing was dominant down low. Chicago lost the first two games of the series.

Things were even worse for Michael Jordan. In game two, he played poorly, and afterward a newspaper reported that before the game he had been seen in a casino in Atlantic City until the early hours of the morning.

The report upset Michael. While he admitted he had been at the casino, he also knew he had been back at his hotel by midnight. He did not appreciate the implication that he had not been ready to play.

He took his anger out on the Knicks. In game three, he led Chicago to a 103–83 win. Then, in game four, he scored 54 points to tie the series at two games. Inspired, the Bulls went on to beat the Knicks in six. It had been a difficult climb up the ladder, but once again, the Bulls, led by Michael Jordan, had made it to the finals.

Their opponents, the Phoenix Suns, had the best record in the league during the regular season. Impressive on paper, that didn't mean much in the finals. The Bulls had Michael Jordan.

In game one, in Phoenix, Michael scored 14 fourth-quarter points. The Bulls won, 100–92. When Chicago took game two, 111–108, the three-peat looked like a sure thing.

But the Suns refused to give up. In game three, in Chicago, they shut down Michael and hung on for a gritty 129–121 victory in triple overtime.

Michael didn't like losing on his home court. In fact, he didn't like losing at all. In game four, he responded with one of the best games of his career, hitting for 55 points and giving the Bulls a three-games-to-one lead. Afterward, Michael reminded everyone, "We're one game away."

The Bulls were still one game away after game five, as the Suns bounced back to beat the Bulls, 108–98. The series went back to Phoenix.

Game six was as tough and hard fought as any in the finals. The Bulls kept creeping ahead only to allow the Suns to draw back close. With only a few minutes left in the game, the Suns jumped out to a 98–94 lead.

Then Michael Jordan got the ball. Every player on the court and every Suns fan in the stands knew what was going to happen, but they were powerless to stop it. Michael Jordan put the ball on the floor, drove to the basket, leaped into the air, and, twisting between two defenders, scored on a layup, bringing the Bulls to within two.

Now Phoenix had the ball. They stalled for as long as they could but had to shoot before the 24-second clock expired. With 14 seconds left in the game, Phoenix guard Dan Majerle threw up an air ball. The Bulls had possession, down by two.

Chicago inbounded the ball to Michael, who took it across half-court. As the defense came out to meet him, he passed the ball to Scottie Pippen on the wing. Pippen threw the ball down low to Horace Grant.

Grant looked for Michael, but Michael was double-teamed. Guard John Paxson stood alone on the perimeter. Grant fired a quick pass to Paxson, who set up just behind the three-point line. He jumped and shot.

Swish! The basket was good! The Bulls had won, 99–98! THREE-PEAT!

The Bulls had done what no NBA team since the 1960s Celtics had done. Much of the credit belonged to Michael Jordan. He had averaged 41 points in the six-game series, an NBA playoff record, and was named MVP for the third straight time. Yet after crying over his first championship and dancing after the second, Michael Jordan was more subdued and reflective this time.

"This championship is something special," he admitted, "because it separates me from Magic and Bird. Neither ever won three straight."

At the end of only his eighth year in the National Basketball Association, Michael Jordan was at the top of his profession. He had just turned 30 years old, yet he had won every award imaginable and led his team to a remarkable string of championships. Basketball historians were beginning to consider Jordan's Bulls one of the greatest teams in NBA history.

As Michael Jordan started his first summer vacation without basketball in two years, he looked forward to getting some rest and, perhaps, setting his sights on some new goals. Life was very, very good. But, as Michael Jordan would soon learn, that could change in an instant.

Chapter Nine:
1993–1994

The News That Shocked the World

In mid-July of 1993, Michael Jordan's father, James, left the family home in North Carolina to visit some friends who lived several hours away. He was driving the brand-new car that Michael had given him. His son's success had allowed him to retire, and James loved to get away by himself. He told his family he would return home in a few days.

A few days passed, and James Jordan did not return. Deloris Jordan began to worry. She hadn't heard from James. While it was not unusual for him to spend several days away from home without calling, as those days stretched into a week, the Jordan family became concerned.

They called everyone they knew but couldn't locate James. They even contacted the North Carolina State Police and asked them to keep an eye out for

James and his car. The media learned that James Jordan was missing, and soon every news broadcast in the state opened with news of his disappearance.

Michael Jordan left Chicago and returned to North Carolina to be close to his family. He was very concerned. James Jordan had been more than a father to Michael. He was also his best friend. James went to almost every Bulls game and often traveled with the team. Michael's teammates had gotten to know James and loved him. When Michael went into a slump or got into trouble, his father was still the first person he went to for advice.

The Jordans sat around the family home, waiting. Every time the phone rang, they jumped, half hoping to hear James Jordan's voice on the other end of the line, half fearing the call would bring bad news.

When they finally got that call, it was the worst news possible. Mr. Jordan's car had been discovered, stripped and abandoned. A body had been found in a creek nearby.

It was James Jordan. From what the police could piece together, James had apparently pulled off the highway late at night to take a nap. He had been attacked. Two 18-year-old boys were soon arrested and charged with James Jordan's murder. Police believed the two boys first robbed, then killed James Jordan.

Michael Jordan was devastated. In an instant, his life had changed. The family held a private, quiet funeral, and Michael went into seclusion. No one heard from him for weeks, though they all expected to see him when the Bulls training camp opened in early October.

Then, October 6, 1993, the Chicago Bulls called a press conference. Just before the conference began, a rumor leaked out that shocked everyone.

Michael Jordan was retiring from basketball!

It was true. Michael and his wife took their places before the microphones at the press conference, and Michael tried to explain why he was retiring.

"I have nothing more to prove in basketball," he said. "I have no more challenges.

"The death of my father made me realize how short life is. I want to give more time to my family."

Despite all the fame and glory his talents had brought him, sometimes it was hard being Michael Jordan. In 1989, he and Juanita had had their first child, a son they named Jeffrey. Two years later another son, Marcus, was born. And in 1992, the couple had a daughter, Jasmine. Michael wanted to spend some time with his family and watch his children grow.

Reporters questioned Michael about his decision. When they asked him if he would ever "un-retire" and return to basketball, Michael just laughed and said, "I never said never." With that, Michael Jordan left the press conference. His basketball career seemed to be over.

At the time of his retirement, there was no question that Michael was one of the best players in NBA history. Only Wilt Chamberlain had been a more prolific scorer, and only the Celtics of the 1960s had won more championships. Perhaps Michael was right. There wasn't much left for him to prove.

But Michael Jordan had a hard time staying retired. He was simply too competitive to sit around or just play golf all day long. Although he loved being with his family, before too long Michael Jordan started considering making a comeback to the world of professional sports.

But it would not be the comeback all NBA fans

were hoping for. Michael Jordan the basketball player wanted to become Michael Jordan the baseball player.

A baseball player? Michael hadn't played baseball since he was a kid. But he and his father had often talked about the possibility, and Michael later said he'd almost left basketball for baseball a few years earlier. Both Michael and his father had wondered how good Michael would have been at baseball if basketball hadn't come along. Now that his father was gone, Michael Jordan decided to find out.

Chapter Ten:
1994-1995

Playing Hardball

Late in 1993, Michael Jordan asked Bulls owner Jerry Reinsdorf, who also owned the Chicago White Sox baseball team, if he could work out with other White Sox players at Comiskey Park. Reinsdorf agreed.

At first, Michael's workouts were a secret, but soon word slipped out that Michael Jordan was considering trading hoops for hardball. When asked, Michael just laughed off the reports and told the press he was simply having fun.

In reality, Michael was testing himself. Hitting against a batting machine under the stands at Comiskey Park, he was trying to learn if he really had the skills to play baseball.

After a month, he had his answer. In January of

1994, Michael called a press conference and announced he was signing with the Chicago White Sox.

"This is something that has been in the back of my mind for a long time," he said to the reporters, "and something that my father and I talked about often."

Michael wasn't the first professional athlete to play two sports. Both Bo Jackson and Deion Sanders played pro football and baseball. Years earlier, star forward Dave Debusschere of the New York Knicks had pitched for the White Sox, and pitcher Gene Conley of the Phillies and Red Sox had played forward for the Celtics.

But none of those other players had ever stopped playing. No one had ever quit one sport to resume playing a sport he'd given up 15 years before. Michael Jordan wasn't like anyone else.

The press scoffed at Michael's announcement. Some speculated that he was just trying to get his name in the paper. Others thought he was being silly. They didn't think anyone, not even a great athlete like Michael Jordan, could make himself into a professional baseball player just because he wanted to. Only a few people thought if anyone could, it was Michael Jordan.

Bulls and White Sox owner Jerry Reinsdorf was one of those people. "Michael likes challenges," he said. "He likes to do what people say he can't do."

Michael Jordan tried to answer his critics, saying, "All I want is a chance to fulfill a dream. If I don't have the skills, I'll walk away from baseball."

Michael joined the White Sox at spring training in Florida. The first time he stepped onto the field in public, he was the biggest story in baseball.

Michael hoped to be able to skip the minor leagues and go directly to the White Sox. But after only a few days of spring training, it became clear that that wasn't going to happen.

The great baseball player Ted Williams once said that hitting a baseball is the hardest thing to do in sports. If that wasn't exactly true, Michael Jordan was proving that hitting a baseball wasn't very easy, either.

While Michael could run and play the outfield, he discovered he had a lot to learn about hitting. The White Sox let Michael play a few exhibition games, but he collected only 3 hits in 20 tries. When they sent him to play in minor league exhibitions, he didn't do much better.

Still, the fact that he could hit at all was encouraging. If he continued to improve, maybe he could play in the major leagues. In the Windy City Classic on April 7, the White Sox played the crosstown Cubs in an exhibition game at Chicago's Wrigley Field. Michael Jordan went 2–5 with two runs batted in (RBIs). He was getting better. After the game, the White Sox assigned him to play for their Double A farm team, the Birmingham (Alabama) Barons in the Southern League.

At age 31, Michael Jordan was the oldest member of the Barons by far. Most of his teammates were in their teens and early twenties. The first few days he was with the team, his teammates were in awe of him and didn't know what to say.

Michael broke the ice with hard work. As soon as his teammates saw that he worked as hard as or even harder than they did, and that he didn't complain about the long bus rides between cities or the fast food they sometimes had to eat on the run, they accepted him. Soon, he was plain old Michael Jordan, outfielder and teammate, instead of Michael Jordan, basketball superstar.

Michael played right field for the Barons. After going 0-for-3 in his first official game on April 8, he collected his first base hit two days later, a single.

The hit sparked a 13-game hitting streak, during which Michael hit .378. All of a sudden, it looked as if Michael Jordan just might play himself into the big leagues!

But after his quick start, Michael cooled off. Soon, his batting average hovered around .200. He was playing well in the field, and when he got on base, he was one of the best base stealers in the league, but he was having trouble hitting. Despite his size and strength, even when he did hit the ball, he usually got only a single.

Michael struggled through much of the season. Toward the end of July, he was hitting only .193. Everyone was saying that Michael Jordan just couldn't cut it as a baseball player.

Then, on July 30, Michael hit his first home run. Later in the same game, he knocked a double. The next day, he pounded out two more hits.

He continued to hit well for the rest of the season. He hit two more home runs and after hitting .260 for August, finished the year with an average of .202, with 3 home runs, 51 RBIs, and 30 stolen bases. Proving he still knew how to play during crunch time no matter what the sport, Michael Jordan was the best clutch hitter on the team.

After the season, some people expected Michael Jordan to give up on baseball. Even Michael admitted that his first season had been "tough, very tough," and that "this game is very humbling." He knew he was a long way from making the major leagues and added, "I'm not sure I can play at that level." But he seemed determined to finish what he had started.

In the off-season, he gave fans in Chicago an opportunity to see him play basketball again. Old Chicago Stadium, the arena where the Bulls had played so successfully under Michael Jordan's leadership, was being torn down and replaced by the new United Center. Michael agreed to play in a charity game with other NBA players to mark the closing of the old building.

Despite not having played a serious game of basketball in over a year, as soon as Michael stepped onto the court, it was as if he had never left. Although the game was just played for fun, and no one played much defense, he still scored 52 points. When Michael left the Chicago Stadium court for the last time, he knelt down and kissed it.

Some fans hoped the game would spark Michael's interest in a return to the NBA. But when the Bulls opened the 1994–95 season in October, Michael Jordan was still a baseball player.

Even without him, the Bulls were still a very good basketball team. Scottie Pippen stepped up as team leader, and any team with Pippen and Horace Grant was still capable of beating anyone. They had made the playoffs in the 1993–94 season, eventually losing to a very good Knicks team in the conference finals. The 1994–95 season promised to be another good one for the Bulls.

Meanwhile, major-league baseball was in turmoil. In the fall of 1994, the players had gone on strike. When they failed to reach a salary agreement with major-league baseball owners, the 1994 World Series was canceled.

The two sides argued all winter without settling

their differences. When spring training opened, the players were still on strike.

Most major-league teams, including the White Sox, decided to field teams of replacement players if the major leaguers didn't return. In February of 1995, Michael Jordan again went to spring training with the Chicago White Sox. His was the most familiar face there. A few weeks into camp, just as the exhibition season was due to begin, the White Sox asked him to become a replacement player.

As much as he wanted to play baseball professionally, Michael Jordan did not want to make the major leagues as some kind of replacement. He wanted to earn the right, as his friends on the White Sox had. He supported the players in the strike and didn't want to risk his friendship with them.

Michael refused to play. When neither the players nor the baseball owners seemed likely to reach an agreement, Michael left spring training. His baseball career was over.

It didn't take long for the rumors to begin that Michael Jordan was going to play basketball again. He dropped in on Bulls practice several times and even took the court. When asked if Michael would be welcomed back, Bulls coach Phil Jackson told reporters, "Michael Jordan is welcome to play with us anytime he wants."

Soon he began practicing in earnest. He wanted to make sure he was ready. On March 18, 1995, Michael Jordan made it official. The Bulls released a brief statement from Michael, consisting of the only two words basketball fans around the world wanted to hear.

"I'm back!"

Chapter Eleven:
1995

"I'm Back!"

Michael Jordan officially returned to the NBA on Sunday, March 19, 1995, when the Bulls played the Indiana Pacers at Market Square Arena in Indianapolis. The game was broadcast across the nation. Every basketball fan in the country was glued to the television set.

When Michael was introduced before the game, the partisan Pacer crowd let loose a mighty roar. They didn't care that he played for the opposition. They were just glad he was playing again. Everyone stood and cheered, drowning out the voice of the announcer. Michael ran onto the court and slapped hands with his teammates. He was back!

Michael looked like the same player he had been when he left the game 21 months before, except for one minor difference — his number. Since he first joined the Bulls, he had always worn number 23. But the Bulls had retired his jersey at the end of the 1993–94 season, so he decided to wear 45, the same number he wore playing baseball.

Coach Phil Jackson put Michael into the starting lineup. The Bulls needed him. Before the season even started, Horace Grant had left the team as a free agent, and the Bulls had struggled all year. Their record was just over .500, 34–32, good enough for only sixth place in the Central Division. The Bulls needed to play well over the remainder of the season to make the playoffs.

The first time Michael touched the ball, he didn't hesitate. He threw up a jumper.

Clang! The ball rattled off the rim.

A few minutes later, Michael shot again. Again, the ball rattled around the rim and fell out.

Then he took another shot. He missed again. Another shot. Another miss.

This wasn't quite the comeback everyone had been hoping for. Michael was out of sync, and so were the Bulls. By halftime, he had made only one shot from the field, and the Bulls trailed.

In the second half, Michael started feeling comfortable again, and the Bulls started remembering what it was like to play with Michael Jordan. Although he still wasn't hitting his shots, he forced the Pacers to pay so much attention to him that other Bulls were left wide open. In the fourth quarter, the Bulls roared back from a 16-point deficit.

At the end of regulation play, the score was tied, 92–92. Michael was exhausted. Although he was in good shape, he wasn't in good *basketball* shape. No amount of practice could compare to the physical challenge of playing a full game in the NBA. In overtime, he simply ran out of steam, and Indiana won, 103–96. Michael Jordan finished with 19 points on 7–28 shooting, 6 rebounds, 6 assists, and 3 steals.

After the game, Michael met with the press for the first time since announcing his return. He told everyone the only reason he had returned: "I just decided I loved the game too much to stay away."

He quickly got used to playing again, and the Bulls got used to having him. In only his fourth game back, against Atlanta, he hit a classic Michael Jordan buzzer-beater, just like old times, to defeat the Hawks. Then, in his fifth game back, he got everyone's attention.

The Bulls played the Knicks at New York's Madison Square Garden, in a game many thought would be a preview of the playoffs. The Knicks had one of the best records in the league, and now that Michael was back, most fans gave the Bulls a good shot at winning another title.

How well he played against the Knicks would give Michael a good idea of how ready he was for the playoffs. The Knicks were still the best defensive team in the league. Even before he had retired, the Knicks had played him tough.

But Michael Jordan had something to prove. Although he had played well since returning, he hadn't quite been the dominant player of before. When he took the court against the Knicks, he wanted to prove to the world that he was back. *Really* back.

For 48 dazzling minutes, basketball fans saw the Michael Jordan of old. No matter how the Knicks defended him, he still found a way to score. He exploded down the baseline for monster dunks and lofted up three-pointers that hit nothing but net.

When the final buzzer sounded, the Bulls had won — and Michael Jordan had scored 55 points! No other player in the league had scored that many points in a game all year! The weary Knicks walked off the court shaking their heads. No player had ever scored 55 points against their team in Madison Square Garden. But Michael Jordan wasn't like any other player.

The Bulls soon got used to winning again, going 13–4 over the final weeks of the season to finish 47–35, good enough for third place in the Central Division. They were only five games behind first-place Indiana.

In the first round of the playoffs, the Bulls played the Charlotte Hornets, who had finished three games ahead of Chicago during the regular season. The Hornets would provide Michael — and the Bulls — with a good test.

Michael passed with flying colors, although it took him three quarters to get going in game one. For most of the game, his teammates struggled, and

Charlotte stayed close. Then Michael Jordan woke up and went to work.

During the final period and overtime, he scored twenty points, including one gravity-defying floating left-handed reverse underhand flip layup off the glass that left the crowd breathless. The Bulls won, 108–100, and after the game, Michael told reporters, "I felt like a shark that smelled blood in the water."

The Bulls went on to defeat the Hornets in four games, earning the right to meet the Orlando Magic in round two.

The Magic had won the Eastern Conference with a record of 57–25. They reminded some people of the Bulls during Michael's first few NBA seasons. Like the old Bulls, the Magic had one player who forced everyone to pay attention.

Big Shaquille O'Neal, over seven feet tall and 300 pounds, anchored the Magic attack. Since coming into the league several years before, he had, in his own way, rivaled Michael Jordan as the most popular player. At first, like the old Bulls, the Magic had struggled. But they had finally acquired some players to give O'Neal some help, like guard

Anfernee "Penny" Hardaway. Like Chicago of a decade before, Orlando was just learning how to win.

The matchup between O'Neal's Magic and Jordan's Bulls was the most eagerly anticipated confrontation of the playoffs.

The first game came down to the last few seconds, and the ball was in Michael Jordan's hands. But as he rushed downcourt to launch a potentially game-winning basket, Magic guard Nick Anderson flashed into his path — and stole the ball! The Magic won, 94–91.

After the game, Anderson got cocky. In reference to Michael, he said, "Number forty-five doesn't explode like number twenty-three used to."

Michael was stung by Anderson's comment. He didn't want anyone to think he wasn't the same player he had been before retirement. So, before game two, he decided to switch back to his old number, 23.

Anderson soon found out what it was like to play against number 23. In game two, Michael made Anderson pay. He hit for 38 points, and the Bulls won, 104–94, to even the series.

But while Michael was playing like his old self, ex-Bull-turned-Magic Horace Grant was asserting himself under the boards and on defense, and Shaquille O'Neal was almost unstoppable. Meanwhile, Scottie Pippen just wasn't hitting his shots. In game three, Michael hit for 40 points, but the Bulls lost, 110–101.

The rest of the Bulls finally got involved in game four. Chicago evened the series at two games apiece, but Orlando would not be denied. In games five and six, they shut down Chicago. Michael Jordan started running out of steam and couldn't do it all by himself. For the first time since the 1989–90 season, a Bulls team that included Michael Jordan lost in the playoffs. The Bulls' season — and Michael Jordan's — was over.

Despite the loss, Michael Jordan had won something almost as valuable as a championship. His inspired play had won back the respect of both his teammates and his opponents. Although he had been away from competitive basketball for nearly two years, he had returned as the most talented and feared player in the game. His future looked nearly as bright as his past.

deadly, and his passing and rebounding also improved. While Jordan was still a threat to soar to the basket and slam down a thunderous jam, the opposition really didn't know what to expect from him anymore. If they guarded him too closely, he made a pass to a wide-open teammate. If they gave him room, he scored at will. In fact, he led the NBA in scoring.

The 1995–96 Bulls were a well-oiled machine. Jordan's return helped teammate Scottie Pippen regain his place as one of the best forwards in the game, and flamboyant Dennis Rodman scooped up nearly every rebound and got the Bulls started with quick outlet passes. Tony Kukoc and Steve Kerr were deadly from the outside, and Coach Jackson kept the Bulls working hard on defense. They finished the regular season 72–10, the best record in league history. But they knew that it would mean nothing unless they won another championship.

In the early rounds of the playoffs, the Bulls were almost unstoppable, losing only once. Not until they reached the finals against the Seattle Supersonics were they tested. After winning the first three games they got sloppy, dropping the next two. Entering game six, an NBA championship was only one win away.

Game six took place on Father's Day. Before the game, Jordan couldn't help but think of his own father. As he told one reporter, "I think about him every day. I'm pretty sure I always will."

But once the game started, Jordan was able to focus on basketball. He and the Bulls took command early and refused to let up. They coasted to an easy 87–75 victory to win their fourth title with Jordan.

After the game he was emotional and broke into tears when he thought about his dad. "I had a lot of things on my heart," he said. "But I had the good fortune to achieve." He did that and more, earning the MVP award for the finals.

With Jordan back, fans and sportswriters began referring to the Bulls as a dynasty. The next year, they cruised through the regular season and again reached the finals, this time facing the Utah Jazz. Utah guard John Stockton and forward Karl Malone were still among the best players in the league. Some observers thought the Jazz had more talent than the Bulls and had a good chance to pull an upset.

But the Bulls had Michael Jordan. With the series

knotted at two games each, Jordan, sick with the flu, crawled out of his sickbed and scored 38 points, including the game-wining three-pointer, as the Bulls won, 90–88.

And in game six the Bulls clawed their way back from a deficit to tie the game in the fourth quarter. With the score at 86–86 and only seconds remaining, Chicago got the ball. Everyone expected Jordan to take the shot, but the experienced Bulls knew that. Steve Kerr drained a three-pointer and the Bulls were champions again.

The Bulls and Jordan began the 1997–98 season looking to win yet another NBA championship, referring to their goal as a "three-peat." But NBA insiders wondered if that was realistic. Jordan and his teammates were getting older, and the competition was getting better.

But beyond that, many expected Bulls management to break up the team at the end of the season. There were rumors that coach Phil Jackson planned to retire, and Jordan indicated that if Jackson left, he didn't expect to return. Forward Scottie Pippen and other Bulls were due new contracts at the end of the year and Bulls management indicated that they didn't believe they could afford to keep the team to-gether. As the season progressed it became clear that the campaign might represent a last hurrah for Jordan and the Bulls.

Although they struggled at times, the Bulls still won the division championship and took aim at the NBA title. In the first two rounds of the playoffs the Bulls easily dispatched the New Jersey Nets and Charlotte Hornets, losing only one game. But in the conference finals against the Indiana Pacers, the Bulls were pushed to the limit. They won in seven games, beating the Pacers, 88–83. But at the end of the game Jordan was so tired that instead of cele-brating, he just bent down, gasping for air. They en-tered the finals against Utah exhausted.

Both teams gave it everything they had. Entering game six in Utah, the Bulls led the series three games to two. They were one game away from an-other championship.

But the Bulls were at something less than full strength. A sore back bothered Scottie Pippen, and the long season had taken a toll on the team. It would be up to Jordan to lead his team to victory.

Just a few moments into the game, Pippen was

forced to the bench when his back started acting up. Jordan took over, scoring 23 points in the first half to keep the Bulls in the game. At the half, they trailed by four points.

Although Pippen returned in the second half, his aching back limited what he could do. Jordan appeared to be running out of steam himself. Early in the fourth quarter he missed five straight shots. Nevertheless, the Bulls hung close, knowing that if they were forced to play a seventh game they would be more fatigued than they already were.

With only 42 seconds left in the game, Jazz guard John Stockton drained a long three-pointer to give the Jazz an 86–83 lead. Bulls fans feared the worst.

But Chicago put the ball in Michael Jordan's hands. Everyone watching knew that if anyone could win the game singlehandedly, it was Jordan.

He dribbled the ball downcourt, probing the defense as the Jazz scrambled to contain him. He hesitated twenty feet from the basket and then made his move.

He spun around guard Bryon Russell and shot toward the hoop. Burly forward Antoine Carr moved over to stop him.

Since Jordan's return from retirement, basketball fans had grown accustomed to seeing him start to drive, then stop and shoot a deadly fadeaway jumper. He rarely attacked the basket anymore.

Antoine Carr may have been thinking the same thing. Only this time, Jordan attacked.

He soared in the air above the bigger player, and before Carr could react, Jordan shoveled a layup off the glass for two points. With 37 seconds remaining, the Bulls trailed by one.

Utah tried to run the clock down as far as possible, then put the ball in the hands of Karl Malone. Jordan reacted immediately.

He spun behind the big man, then reached in and tipped the ball away. Jordan had stolen the ball!

The clock was ticking down. The Jazz sprinted downcourt to stop the Bulls. Jordan streaked toward the basket. Fifteen feet short of the basket, he stopped. Bryon Russell tried to skid to a stop and stick with Jordan, but Jordan took a short step back and then lofted a seventeen-foot jump shot. Russell, too late, went up to stop the shot.

The ball seemed to hang in the air forever as Jordan dropped to the ground and kept his hands in the precise position they were when he had released the shot. The ball dropped through the hoop.

The Bulls led! Jordan had hit the last shot!

The Jazz had time to throw up a desperation shot in the final second, but it missed the basket. The Bulls won, 87–86, their third straight championship. Jordan's 45-point performance, capped by his last-shot heroics, made the game perhaps the most memorable of his career. "It just keeps getting sweeter every time," he said afterward.

Chapter Thirteen
2001–2003

Jordan's Finale

In the weeks and months that followed this historic Bulls three-peat, rumors began to spread that the game-winning shot against Utah would be the last of Jordan's career. Coach Jackson did decide to retire, and the Bulls decided to rebuild. At the same time, a labor dispute between the players' union and the NBA owners caused the start of the season to be delayed by a lockout.

Every day the lockout went on, it seemed more and more likely that Jordan would retire. There were reports that he wasn't even working out anymore.

Finally, on January 6 the labor dispute was settled. Jordan flew to Chicago and told his teammates of his decision. Then, on January 13, he made it official.

"After a great deal of thought," he said, "I have

decided to retire from basketball." The Jordan era appeared over.

Over the next year Jordan spent time doing what he wanted to do — golfing, spending time with his family, and taking care of his business interests. He even purchased a small portion of the Washington Wizards of the NBA.

There was immediate speculation that Jordan would mount another comeback. But he laughed off those suggestions, insisting that he had no plans to return.

But in the spring of 2001, there were persistent rumors that Jordan was working out again and playing basketball. He didn't deny the rumors, but insisted that he had put on a few pounds and simply wanted to get back in shape.

No one was fooled. As spring turned into summer it became clear that Jordan was ready to return. When he sold his share of the Wizards, it became apparent the rumors were true, as NBA rules prohibit a player from owning a portion of the team.

Many people thought Jordan was making a huge mistake. The Wizards were terrible, and at age thirty-eight, even Jordan's supporters had to admit that there was little chance that he could come back and resume his place as the best player in basketball. Many criticized Jordan for his decision, believing he was returning only for the money and that it was certain to damage his reputation as the greatest player in the game.

Jordan didn't care. He missed the competition and challenge of playing. He had also discovered that he hadn't really enjoyed retirement.

In his first few weeks back in the NBA, it seemed as if Jordan's critics were right. The Wizards were terrible and won only two of their first eleven games. And Jordan wasn't playing very well. His knees were bothering him, and he often had to sit out practices. He rarely went to the basket, and his patented fadeaway jump shot seemed to have deserted him. The comeback appeared to have been a mistake.

But the bigger mistake has always been in underestimating Jordan. Suddenly, he and the Wizards started playing better. They won eight straight, and Jordan appeared to be getting his game back.

As 2001 turned into 2002, Jordan turned back the

clock. In back-to-back games he exploded for a total of 96 points. His jump shot was falling and his quickness returned as he got his legs in game shape. Moreover, his young teammates began to learn to play with him, to expect the passes that few other players in the game could make, and to take advantage of the space on the floor that opened up when the opposition found that they had to start double-teaming Jordan again.

On January 3 he scored 25 first-half points against the Bulls, including the 30,000th point of his NBA career. He was just the fourth player to reach that milestone, joining Kareem Abdul-Jabbar, Wilt Chamberlain, and Karl Malone.

But Chicago fought back in the second half, and with fifteen seconds left, Bulls guard Ron Mercer swooped in for a layup. Jordan went up with him.

And up. And up. At the top of his leap, he reached for the ball.

He didn't block the shot. He *caught* it. And when he came back down to earth it was clear to everyone that Michael Jordan could still do things on a basketball court that few others could.

The crowd went wild, and the Wizards hung on to

win. After the game, a smiling Jordan admitted, "I can jump pretty high."

But all was not well for Jordan. Though he continued to play hard throughout January and February, he was plagued by continuous pain in his right knee. Doctors at first suspected it was tendonitis. When nothing they did seemed to help, Jordan knew it was time to take a closer look.

At the end of February, he went into the hospital for exploratory surgery. Jordan was fearful doctors would fine a career-ending injury. To his relief, the problem turned out to be loose cartilage, a condition that can often be corrected. Surgery was performed, and Jordan was placed on the Wizards' injured list.

Soon after the surgery, rumors began circulating that Michael Jordan was going to announce his retirement. Speculation lasted days, until at last Jordan put all rumors to rest. He would return to the game as soon as his recovery allowed.

Jordan worked hard to get back in top form in the months that followed. When the 2002 season began, he made it clear he was ready, emotionally and physically.

"My love for the game of basketball continues to drive my decision [to play]," he stated. "I am feeling very strong, and feel that the steps I took in the off-season have allowed me to return to the game in great condition."

Jordan went into the 2002–2003 season ranked first in NBA history in scoring average, with 31.0 points per game. He was also second in steals, fourth in total points and field goals made, and fifth in free throws made. Anything he did in the upcoming months would only add to those already impressive totals.

Jordan had originally opted to rest his knee during the preseason and watch the games from the sidelines. But in a preseason game on October 21, he came off the bench with less than eight minutes left in the second quarter. In typical fashion, he sank a turnaround jumper three minutes after entering the game. He drained three more in the third quarter for a total of eight points in fourteen minutes of play.

Coming off the bench was something new for Jordan — but it was something he knew he was going to have to get used to. His knee wasn't one hundred percent yet, and although he was in good shape, other younger players were in better condition. So for the first time in years, he would be the strong sixth man on the team until he was truly ready to take his place among the starters.

Still, joining the game midway was not easy. During his first outing, against the Toronto Raptors on October 30, he couldn't seem to find his rhythm. He took to the floor with less than four minutes left in the first quarter. When he left after having played for twenty-five minutes, he had hit only four shots out of fourteen. He also went zero for two from the foul line. Perhaps the most telling of all was the slam dunk that clanged off the rim. The Wizards lost 74–68 — and sports networks replayed the flubbed dunk over and over while speculating that Jordan was past his prime.

Jordan rebounded the next night, scoring twenty-one points in as many minutes in a win against the Boston Celtics. Yet he still seemed off his game. By the last week of November, he hadn't moved from substitute to starter or reached the thirty-point mark, something that had once been so easy for him.

It may be that Jordan could see the writing on the wall. Or perhaps he simply wanted to end speculation over his career. Whatever the reason, on Thanksgiving Day, Michael Jordan called a press conference and announced that when the 2002–2003 season was over, he would retire from the game.

Jordan had made this announcement twice before in his career, once in 1993 and again in 1999, only to come out of retirement and rejoin the game he loved. This time, however, he meant it, saying there was "zero chance" that he would return.

"I just want to fulfill my year and enjoy it," he insisted.

The previous two times Jordan had retired, the basketball world had gone into a tailspin. This time, however, reaction was more subdued. Many people even congratulated the star player on making a sound decision, one that was good for him and good for the team.

But Jordan's actual retirement was still months away. Two days after the announcement, Coach Collins moved Jordan from the bench to the starting lineup for a game against Philadelphia. In his first game as a starter, Jordan played thirty-seven minutes and scored sixteen points.

In the weeks that followed, Jordan's average playing time edged up close to thirty minutes per game. His average points-per-game increased as well, including a season-high 33 in mid-December.

Unfortunately, the Wizards were not doing as well. By the end of 2002, their record stood at thirteen wins, seventeen losses. Things seemed to be improving at the start of the new year, however, when they added four straight wins. The second of these games saw the return of vintage Michael Jordan.

The Wizards faced the Pacers on January 4. The teams were evenly matched throughout and the game went into two overtimes. When the match finally ended with a win in the Wizards' pocket, there was no doubt in anyone's mind that Michael Jordan had tipped the scales in his team's favor. In fifty-three minutes of play, he scored forty-one points, twenty of which came in the fourth quarter and double overtime. It was his last two points, both free throws made in the second overtime, that put the Wizards in the lead for good.

"Tonight, with the highest of things at stake, my

game came to me," Jordan said afterward. "Hope-fully, this is just the start of something big."

But Jordan's dreams of an upswing for himself and his team were not to come true. In his next twenty games, he would pass the thirty-point mark only twice — and in one game in which he played thirty-seven minutes, he was held to a mere four baskets.

Meanwhile, the Wizards lost eleven of those twenty games. By mid-March, it was clear to basket-ball followers that the Wizards would not be playoff contenders that year.

With retirement a month away and no shot at a championship, some players might have chosen to take it easy. Not Michael Jordan. He pushed him-self even harder, playing longer and longer games and routinely adding twenty or more points to the scoreboard. And in early April, he showed people that he still had what it took to make great plays.

The Wizards were playing the Celtics in Boston on April 6. The score seesawed back and forth through much of the game. In the final minute, the Celtics were up by two and seemed sure to win.

Then, with forty-three seconds on the clock, Jordan drained a fourteen-foot jump shot. The game went into overtime.

Again, the minutes ticked down. With less than a minute remaining, the score was 98–97 in Boston's favor. Enter Michael Jordan. This time he set up teammate Christian Laettner for a wide-open shot. Laettner hit the bucket — and the Wizards took the game, 99–98.

Six games later, on April 16, Jordan wore his Wizards uniform for the last time in an away game against the 76ers. The Philadelphia crowd greeted him with a standing ovation that lasted three minutes. They knew that they were watching the last game of the best player basketball had ever known.

It was to be a bittersweet finale for Michael Jordan. Some of his plays, such as a commanding one-handed dunk in the second quarter, earned him a roar of approval from the crowd. But there were as many missed shots as there were solid plays. Twice Jordan made a move to the basket for a classic lay-up only to have the ball hit the rim and bounce off.

He also bobbled an alley-oop pass and threw another pass that was picked off easily.

Unfortunately, the rest of the Wizards were playing badly as well. With nine and a half minutes left in the game, they were down by twenty-one. Jordan was sitting on the bench in his warm-ups, waiting for it to end.

Then the crowd started chanting, "We want Mike! We want Mike!" For more than six minutes, Coach Collins ignored them. But with two and a half minutes remaining, Jordan stood up, removed his sweats, and took the floor one last time. He played for less than a minute. His last shot as a professional basketball player was a free throw.

He sank the bucket, waved to the crowd a final time, and left. He had played twenty-eight minutes of the game, chalked up fifteen points, four rebounds, and four assists.

Those final game statistics say little of a career that spanned nearly two decades. Michael Jordan joined the NBA when he was twenty-three years old. He was forty when he played his last game. He played fifteen seasons, 41,011 minutes in 1,072 games. During those games, he had scored an astounding 32,292 points, giving him the third highest total in NBA history after Kareem Abdul-Jabbar and Karl Malone. His final career average of 30.12 places him in first, just above Wilt Chamberlain. He won six NBA Championships, was named NBA MVP five times, and NBA Finals MVP six times.

Off the court, Michael Jordan remains deeply committed to charitable children's causes. He actively supports the Boys & Girls Clubs of America and the Special Olympics, among others. He continues to donate his time and money to programs aimed at strengthening families.

Even though he's no longer on the court, basketball will continue to be a part of his life as he takes a role behind the scenes with the Wizards.

"Basketball has been my life," Jordan said shortly after his last game. "No way you would ever have come in contact with me without the game of basketball. No way would I have been in contact with a lot of other people without the game of basketball. It gave me an outlet. . . . It taught me a lot of things about life in terms of respect, hard work,

Matt Christopher®

Lance Armstrong

Kobe Bryant

Jennifer Capriati

Terrell Davis

Julie Foudy

Jeff Gordon

Wayne Gretzky

Ken Griffey Jr.

Mia Hamm

Tony Hawk

Grant Hill

Ichiro

Derek Jeter

Randy Johnson

Michael Jordan

Mario Lemieux

Tara Lipinski

Mark McGwire

Greg Maddux

Hakeem Olajuwon

Shaquille O'Neal

Alex Rodriguez

Curt Schilling

Briana Scurry

Sammy Sosa

Venus and
Serena Williams

Tiger Woods

Steve Young

The #1 Sports Series for Kids

Read them all!

*Originally published as *Crackerjack Halfback*